THE BLESSINGS OF THE DARK

SINGING HAWK

BALBOA.PRESS
A DIVISION OF HAY HOUSE

Balboa Press books may be ordered through booksellers or by contacting:

Balboa Press
A Division of Hay House
1663 Liberty Drive
Bloomington, IN 47403
www.balboapress.com
1 (877) 407-4847

Scripture quotations marked NIV are taken from the Holy Bible, New International Version®. NIV®. Copyright © 1973, 1978, 1984 by International Bible Society. Used by permission of Zondervan. All rights reserved.

Scripture quotations marked NLT are taken from the Holy Bible, New Living Translation, copyright © 1996, 2004, 2007. Used by permission of Tyndale House Publishers, Inc. Carol Stream, Illinois 60188. All rights reserved.

ISBN: 978-1-9822-4578-8 (sc)
ISBN: 978-1-9822-4579-5 (e)

Print information available on the last page.

Balboa Press rev. date: 03/31/2020

Human beings are taught to fear darkness. By whom and for what purpose is beyond the scope or interest of this book as, ultimately and to the surprise of the reader, such information is of little practical value. Darkness is a tool that allows the seeker to find the light and appreciate the light innately and completely. While many well intended people proclaim their affection and subservience to the light both actions demonstrate an inaccurate view of the light and a life of imbalance. It is the intention of this book to introduce tools and wisdom to the reader to allow the reader to take the next step on their journey towards balance, harmony, and unity... the path of darkness.

Those who are not ready for this information will readily dismiss the truths and concepts of this book as bunk and think me a fool. Those who are actively seeking for truth will find this book brilliant and attribute the same to its author. Those who are awake, however, will find this book as basic and common sense. I look forward to a time when the truths of this book – and its concepts – are basic to all!

CONTENTS

I WENT TO KILL GOD

I was done. I was frustrated. I felt as if I were bound to my perceived and self imposed social status as an American Untouchable by Gleipnir as I found that the more I struggled the stronger I was bound to my frustration. Despite being endowed with gifts that allowed me to learn quickly and channel universal wisdom innately I was extremely tired. I was working way too many hours for far too little pay for multiple decades while being a single father who graduated college with honors. All of the time I spent earning the highest grade in the class and differentiating my resume from my coworkers and fellow students did nothing to assist me in the marketplace and I was mentally exhausted and every day looked the same without hope for a better tomorrow. I did the best I could to be the best parent I could possibly be for my child but I wanted better for my child and I found myself spiraling in to a chasmic depression. I had been here before but this time I was done. I was fully and completely defeated and I needed an immediate change.

Suicide was not an option as suicide truly does not do much for anyone… and not for the programmed reasons the reader is checking off in their mind. Truthfully self murder is no more or no less a "sin" then the murder of anything or anyone else. Suicide, in effect, is essentially very similar to using substances, sex, or any other form of distraction to avoid feelings, circumstances, or "reality" as it is only temporary and the issues that are being avoided remain and fester.

As a medium, I have interacted with disincarnates (souls without a physical body) who have committed suicide and they typically report the following generalization. The body – or meat puppet as I prefer to call it – does an extraordinary job of attenuating (reducing or eliminating the signal energy) most of the infinite amount of information that bombards you without pause. For those who doubt the efficacy of such attenuation consider this… at this moment EVERY television program, radio program, cell phone call, citizen band QSO, amateur radio CQ, police chatter, etc. is happening around you each and every moment but the reader is unaware of such. Even when the reader is able to perceive such event, it is only with the aid of a down converter or transceiver that allows the reader to experience the event within the very limited range of human "senses" and, even then, it is typically one at a time.

It is due to this attenuation that humans are afforded the illusion of separation and individualism and all the good and bad that comes with it but of the attenuation is dissolved once the soul is disincarnate. In other words… you feel everything in all its rawness and without filter which translates to a horrible situation in which the reasons you committed suicide becoming immediately and intensely real without filter or ability to hide. Opioid addicts will understand this as being dope sick whereas alcoholics will appreciate this as having a hangover while all the reasons you self medicated to avoid are knocking loudly. Such drug analogies pale in comparison to the feelings of the soul who commits suicide as they are suddenly faced with not only the feelings they were seeking to escape but they also feel ALL of the feelings of the loved ones they left behind and who are in shock at the discovery of the self murder.

So, in spite of the programming saying that suicide is the coward's way out or some other judgment based nonsense, suicide is not the best path as it succeeds in only postponing the lesson the soul incarnated to experience and is a near guaranteed way to ensure another round in the incarnation cycle. In fact, I have passed this wisdom to souls who are contemplating suicide and have been successful in swaying their decision by noting how terrible it would be to have to recreate the circumstances that brought the soul to its lesson… since you have made it this far… why not finish your hell now? Or, as the common adage relays, if you find yourself in the middle of "Hell"… keep going!

For the record and in an effort to prevent anyone from saying that my book is the reason for their loved one's suicide… I do NOT condone suicide and I am NOT – in ANY way shape, form, or manner real, implied, or imagined – endorsing or promoting suicide. If you read the words I have composed and channeled, you will see that I use my understanding to do all I can to persuade those with suicidal idealization or intention to not move forward with their plan so should your loved one commit suicide, don't come looking for me.

Knowing this and knowing that I did NOT want to repeat a similar set of circumstances to bring me to a similar point of understanding… it was not suicide I wanted… I wanted non-existence.

Non-existence, or soul death, is not a possibility that I am sure exists but at this time I was doing my best to fit within a religious paradigm and knowing that the "God" presented in the Bible is a ruthless tyrant who will condemn the entirety of a species to eternal pain and suffering for the mistake of a single person – a person whose existence cannot be verified… I was pretty sure this method would be my way out so off I went.

Where I went or how I got there is of little importance but it was not long before I arrived at an indescribably beautiful garden and found myself looking at an immaculate sculpture that was on a stage. The wonder and beauty of the garden was intoxicating but I was not there for balance, harmony, or healing so I forcibly and gruffly demanded "God" to appear. The statue began to animate and it was show time. I knew there was no way I could defeat "God" in combat and my fate was as good as sealed so I manifested ALL of my frustration, hate, self loathing, pain, misery, and darkness to become as threatening as possible. My fire burned with the intensity of a million suns and I found myself both amazed and frightened by my strength but there was no turning back now… I issued my threat with the darkest words and intention I could muster and awaited "God's" attack.

I watched as "God" looked at me, took a few steps, smiled, and said, "You are a great father. Not just to your child but to the world." I was dumbfounded. Here I was purposely, intentionally, and wantingly committing a "sin" that is FAR worse the anything the Bible reports Lucifer did and nothing. No action, no disdain, no soul death, nothing… not even a mocking tone or condescending body gesture. In fact, the ONLY thing that "God" did was bless me. "God's" unconditional love was so profound and penetrated me so deeply that my fire was extinguished and I returned to my body with a new outlook on life and with hope.

Who Cares Analysis	This is a great story but who cares? How does this – unverifiable and implausible incident – matter to anything in the reader's life? These are fair questions and introduces my Who Cares Analysis that I use in all my presentations to ensure proper conveyance of the intended message. The entire story presented in this section is indeed unverifiable as I cannot prove it happened anymore than I can prove many of my childhood memories or memories of the inbetween stage. Hopefully the reader is able to dismiss the admitted implausibility of the story and appreciate how I learned about the true God and its love. This love is truly unconditional and is NOT solely for me or solely for the people who buy my books and listen to my banter… it is universal and available to everyone at ALL times and on ALL paths.

MY VISIT TO CHRISTIAN HELL

My encounter with "God" left me with a bevy of questions. The experience did not go as planned and I, thankfully, did not encounter the judgmental despot that is the controlling force of fear in organized religion which led me to question what I was allowing myself to be programmed with and reflect on my own personal experiences and memories.

I suppose I am different than most others as most people seem completely oblivious to past lives (more aptly and hereafter called past experiences), memories of the time in-between experiences, and ANY messages or teachings from the other side but I have always had those memories. I, in fact, recall being VERY happy as a disincarnate being and was extremely at ease with my life on the other side. I can still see my essence happily serving the growth of others and basking in the energy of the higher realms. While I cannot seem to recall the face of the "person" who asked me to incarnate, I recall being ecstatic that I was going to be of service to the "forgotten" – those who have forgotten themselves and are disorientated in themselves. I do not recall all of the planning that occurred before the experience but I do recall the last thing I heard before I entered this experience... "It doesn't matter what happens to you. What matters is how you deal with it".

Like the happy lark portrayed as the Fool in just about any tarot or oracle deck, I happily took the next step without looking and felt well prepared for the challenges I was about to immerse myself in. I dove in to my incarnation and found myself the ward of well intended addicts with cash flow and emotional challenges and I suffered from health challenges that were, in part, related to the maternal substance abuse. I was even "treated" with highly toxic medication as the attending physicians did not understand – in those days – that my ailment was withdrawal. I recall having to wear leg braces, having a benign tumor removed from my arm, and hushed conversations that my mother was suffering from Munchhausen Syndrome by Proxy – a condition that allowed her to gain attention because I was always sick. Then came school.

I was a target. My good nature, desire to be of service, and lack of desire or intention to hurt others with a weak ego made me a prime target for dark teachers – those who are skilled at inflicting pain, suffering, and the like. I did my best to fit in but while my classmates were finding immense pleasure in describing – at great length – and demonstrating the finer points of passing gas and the never-ending variety of uses for dried nasal mucus, I was studying religions, mythologies, and demonstrated a keen interest in hard and soft sciences including astrology, astronomy, analysis, and information technology. I did my best to fit in but was different in every way possible and I eventually learned that being from the same church could help with status and gain friends so I did my best to bury my innate knowledge and embrace another point of view.

While many of the lessons being taught in organized religion made no sense to me and seemed to be a highly contradictory concept of fear based "love", I studied and rose in the ranks and, very quickly, I found myself assisting in Bible study, Sunday School, and serving as an usher. Even while under the influence of this mindset and doing the best I could to be a good member, however, I had an issue with various concepts of eternal punishment and would pray to "God" for two things, (1) that I NOT be raptured when the time comes as I wanted to remain here to help guide the lost and (2) to grant my mother a temporary reprieve from her torment in Hell as she committed the unforgivable sin (as irrational as this would be to a being of unconditional love) of suicide. I had come full circle even from a different perspective.

So then it occurred sometime thereafter – I honestly cannot recall when and such detail is ultimately of little importance and does not matter – that I dreamt that I awoke in Christian Hell. I found that I was in a house that was surrounded by demons who were trying to get in to get me. The realization that I was in Hell was terrifying as the stories of the place are not good and based upon the sheer size of the armada that was there to collect me... I was in trouble.

The first thing I wondered was why I was there... I am a good person... a Lightworker and I should not be here. Sure I have made some less than optimal decisions during my growth challenges but I have passed such challenges so why am I here? Next, and more importantly, I pondered, how do I get out? I took stock of my skill set and noted I have various titles including Reiki Master, Akashic Reader, spiritual counselor, and the sort but I did not see how or which of these titles were going to help me get out.

I analyzed all I knew about demons to pinpoint any possible exploitable weakness and the answer came back as light. The dark cannot touch the light - without the light's express or implied permission - so then the next question is... where do I find light in Hell? As a Lightworker and Reiki "master" light is my ally and I noticed that "Hell" had a low – but existent – bioluminescence so then I did what any reasonable Reiki Master would do and I used the Light of Hell to set up energy boundaries around the structure of the house so that the demons could not penetrate the house. This strategy worked but it rapidly became obvious that demons are not limited to the dimensions of x and y as they can fly so they quickly began attacking from z.

I began using Reiki as a laser beam that I shot from my hands which meant that I needed to see the potential breach to seal it which was a slow and tedious process which left my flanks exposed which were, almost immediately, attacked. I decided to up my Reiki and began to envision the entire home filled with light from outside of the home thereby protecting the entire house. This worked but I understood that this made me a prisoner of the house as I was still surrounded by demons who were unaffected and unimpressed by my defense and they just needed to wait for me to leave the house or tire and I would be collected. I needed a more permanent solution.

As I pondered my situation, it occurred to me that Reiki is beyond space and time and I could easily send Reiki back in time to shield me from this ever happening and then I wondered... why am I using a religious instrument like Reiki when I, as a part of God, am much more powerful than that and I do not need to constrain myself within the limitations of a pseudoreligion. I did not need Reiki to protect myself in time as I could go back in time and prevent the original demon from existing. It occurred to me that demons were nothing more than negative thought forms that were created and are kept in existence by the collective fears of other God parts who were still in the process of awakening.

I attuned my light to a level that was strong enough to prevent any demon from touching or getting near me but soft enough as not to harm them and then sent out an energy pulse that, literally, blew the walls off and the house shattering it into, seemingly, millions of shards as if it were made out of glass.

At that moment, the energy shifted drastically. The fear and darkness that moments ago were highly palatable suddenly seems lighter and brighter. The demons that were running around like crazed crackheads at a money spill all calmed and seemed somber... if not reverent. I approached the head demon and announced that I can wipe out the entire demon race from existence with a single thought but I will not as they have a function to perform and right to exist. I blessed them for the service they perform but forbade them from ever bothering me again and I found that I was very happy and I awoke... happy to have had – and overcome – that growth challenge.

In Hell, I had experienced a full gambit of dark emotions; i.e. fear, terror, abandonment, and self doubt and had overcome the emotions by going inside and connecting to my true self. I had gone from seeing the demons as a threat that needed to be annihilated to a tool needed to help those find their answers inside. I had gone from cursing God for putting me there to thanking God for putting me there as it was the optimal reconnection tool for me.

Who Cares Analysis	Again I have presented another story that is without validation which, again, begs the question, who cares? This section was presented to outline a sample of the bevy of spiritual "tools" and titles I have access to and how ineffective and unnecessary they were when I needed them as they are no more powerful or effective than the energy I allot to them. Whether or not the reader believes in organized religion or Hell is without regard to the intended message and the reader should not get lost in their programmed dissonance that they miss the message.

FIGHTING MY DEMON – MY FIRST TOOL OF RECONNECTION

Being poor in a poor country is without shame but being the poorest of the poor in a rich country is not fun… a lesson I experienced in foster care. By the time I became full ward of the state I had endured quite a bit growth challenges and was trying to balance issues including physical abuse, mental abuse, bullying, anorexia, bulimia, self loathing, self mutilation, self hate, and abandonment to name a few. I did the best I could to be of a "general euthymic attitude" but I felt poisoned as the unbridled anger that typically accompanies structural strain was always simmering just below the surface… waiting and wanting to explode. The details of the maladies mentioned herein are not important as they are simply the conditions I needed for my growth. Of course I did not realize that at the time so it was with much trepidation that I found myself battling a demon without the aid of anyone or anything.

I was no slouch during this period as my anorexia, bulimia, and self loathing had transformed my body in to a lean, strong, and well defined machine that was fueled by my anger and hate. I seemed impervious to physical pain and healed extremely quickly. I earned an advanced belt in martial arts but was kicked out the of the program as the instructor wisely understood that I was not there to learn "self defense" or win trophies rather I was there to learn the best ways to defeat all comers. The instructor was able to see that the techniques I displayed were NOT what was taught in the school and the stuff I was doing came from me channeling some of the dark skills I developed in a previous experience. Afterwards I found that I could channel my reservoir of anger in to weight lifting and I quickly found myself lifting multiples of my body weight which resulted in me becoming a very strong dark warrior whose aura was so dark that people would literally scream and jump out of my aura's reach. I thought I was invincible… the demon showed me otherwise.

It came one night without warning and without mercy. It was large in stature, terrorizing in appearance, and yielded an unlimited cache of weapons that maximized and extended its insatiable hunger for pain and suffering and I was its prey and defenseless. No matter how I tried to attack or evade, the demon was a step ahead constantly mocking me, belittling me, and laughing at me. The demon took great pleasure in slicing my soul in to small, pcio sized pieces and throwing each piece in to an unimaginably painful fire that incinerated me for the sole purpose that the demon could reconstitute me in order to repeat the process. I felt EVERY punch, every slice, and every flame without filter. I hoped and prayed that I would find refuge in oblivion each time I was rendered essenceless but there was no reprieve therein as I found the demon's fiery iced grip would always be there with its hate oozing from its laser sharp claws to keep me from having ANY moment or thought of easement.

There was no way out and no peace for me as whenever I would fall asleep... the demon was there patiently and eagerly waiting for me. I cannot recall how long I suffered this before it occurred to me that I DID have some control over the demon as it would not be able to attack me if I did not fall asleep. So I did the only thing I could do... I became an insomniac. Again, I do not recall how long this lasted but even with my insomnia fueled by fear I found that my thought process was flawed as now the demon could attack me while awake as my exhausted mind began to lose the differentiation between being "awake" and asleep. I was approaching compete adrenal fatigue and did not have a way out so there was only one place to go... inside.

Somewhere from within the utter and impenetrable prison of darkness that I was fully immersed in came a tiny flash of inspiration... a tiny vision of hope... a fleeting image which was all I had so I decided to listen to it. The vision reminded me of who and what I was and encouraged me to return to myself through meditation... a practice I had stopped in my attempt to fit in. Then, as now, I am not one who can sit there and ohm as doing so bores me completely but in this case I was so exhausted that I immediately collapsed in to a "pose" and rediscovered and reconnected to the light that is within me... that is me. It had been a while since I had seen myself in my native state. In fact the last time I was able to recall seeing myself like this is when I anchored myself in to the meat puppet that is my vehicle in this experience and remarked to myself how bright it was in the womb. It did not occur to me at that moment that the light I saw in the darkness of the womb is the same blessed flash of inspiration that I had recently encountered in my prison of darkness... it was ME!

I remembered that I am immortal, I am flawless, and I am unable to be hurt, controlled, or limited without my consent and I DO NOT consent! I snapped awake and was refreshed and, for the first time in a LONG time... I was ready to go to sleep!

As expected and hoped for, the demon was there waiting for me and I slaughtered the demon without allowing even a scratch to myself. I found the roles had reversed and the demon was powerless to do anything against my righteous revenge and liberation fueled onslaught. I was completely and wholly victorious and feel in to a well deserved and hard earned sleep for the first time in what felt like an eternity.

It was about a week later, if I recall correctly, when a startling understanding suddenly entered in to my consciousness as I sat on the couch smugly recanting my self ordained awesomeness... the reason the demon was so successful in knowing how to defeat me is because the demon is my best friend who has walked with and trained with me many times before. Not only did that revelation immediately humble me but I also understood that not only did the demon feel every pain it caused me but it also was THE reason for my flash of insight as its merciless onslaught was the only thing that was able to create the smallest of kinks in the ocean of darkness I chose and shielded myself in which allowed for my insight to enter... something the demon and I had planned as a contingency during my life plan.

| **Who Cares Analysis** | This section presents some of the basic tenants of this book which are designed to educate the reader in the fact that ALL of existence is benevolent and is working for your betterment. Also, in this section, I outlined a sampling of the growth challenges I experienced during my childhood during my current experience. It is important to note that such items were shared NOT for sympathy or to compare scars but to demonstrate another universal truth… you can overcome anything <u>you choose</u> to overcome. |

WHAT DOES IT MEAN TO IGNORE THE SIGNS?

My child has a fascination with Denver despite probably never having been there in this experience. I am not sure if the fascination is due to a past life experience, my story of my experience in Denver, or a mixture of both but it was the Holiday season and I had time off from work so it seemed like a good time to go. Denver was not too far from Sedona and it seemed to be a simple path for arrival... Sedona to Albuquerque and then Albuquerque to Denver. I'm sure there is more to it but that was the path. We found a hotel that was not too unreasonable, packed, and got on the road.

It sucked! The ENTIRE road from Sedona to Albuquerque was nothing but a freak winter storm that consisted of all variants of frozen and near frozen water, fog, and high winds which was EXTREMELY odd for the time of the year and the area. No big deal, I thought, as an ex-Alaskan, I have been in worse and I pressed on. The storm – unrelentingly – accompanied us throughout the ENTIRE 350 mile distance, give or take, and I got a bit frazzled and finally pulled off the highway to get gas in Albuquerque an exit or so before the turn to Denver.

I decided to take some time to balance my mind so I slowly inspected some of the Southwestern curios for sale in the store when something caught my attention... the news. I stopped watching and listening to the "news" some time ago as there really is nothing

"news worthy" and I have NO use for the fear-mongering and celebrity worshiping tripe that passes for modern "news" and I found it odd that the news would catch my attention so I watched. What I saw was a CLEAR message that going to Denver was NOT in my best interest as the road to Denver was suffering an unprecedented storm and I was likely to be stuck on a closed highway for an untold amount of time should I press forward. I explained the circumstances to my child who was disappointed but, wisely, agreed it was best to turn around so, begrudgingly, we did.

Surprisingly, the road back to Sedona was COMPLETELY clear. There seemed to be NO trace of the storm that accompanied us the entire time towards Albuquerque with the expectation of the occasional wet spot on the road. My child took note of this and mentioned how odd it was that the storm was gone the moment we turned around so I wondered why we were not supposed to go to Denver as I was a bit irritated at the time and cost of the wasted trip. Well it was not long before we found out.

We had planned on doing some sightseeing in Denver and had a rudimentary plan which would have put us in the same time and area as a shooting that occurred that weekend in Denver. So while I cannot say that we would have been victims of the shooting... I am appreciative that spirit spent a LOT of time to get my attention and prevent us from being in the line of fire even if it took them several hundreds of miles for me to get the message. I also received the message that had I, stubbornly, decided to press on – a trait I am noted for – then spirit would have continued to attempt to prevent this future possibility by either giving me car trouble or getting me in to an accident so that I would not be in the area at the time of the shooting.

Admittedly, there is no way for me to definitively discern the outcome of the trip since we turned around and I am sure there are those out there poo-pooing the weather conditions as normal circumstances and are attempting to "scientifically" dismiss all of the signs. The fun and paradoxical consideration is, however, that had I ignored the signs, I may not be here to relay this concept in this book.

Who Cares Analysis	The reader may have noticed that I tend to be very "conservative" when it comes to names, gender, or details but all of the sudden here I am naming dropping Sedona and Albuquerque in nearly every paragraph… what gives? Honestly? Nothing. While it is true that I enjoy the American Southwest, the only reason for the name dropping is to paint a picture in the reader's mind so that the reader is more attuned to the message presented in the story. The universe is ALWAYS giving you the signs you need to help you achieve what it is you choose to achieve but we can postpone receipt if we fail to listen.

HOW CAN A DEMON BE A FRIEND?

There is no easy way to say this but if this is question you are asking then you have been lied to and are being manipulated. Again, by whom and for what reason is beyond the scope and interest of this book but if you are thinking that demons are bad then you really need to consider the following words.

Many religions present the spiritual realms as a highly stratified social structure in which the top is a monarchical despot whose word and actions are beyond reproach simply because you are programmed to allow the top to do whatever the despot chooses without question and regardless of the actions of the despot. Historically this is seen in the concept of calling the King a Sire as the King – or another direct member of the "royal" bloodline – will grant themselves a Machiavellian exclusion from the "law" so that they are free to sire – or more honestly called rape – any of their constituents that grabs their attention at any time... typically first. This legal exclusion is called a "Royal Right" and its administration is highly prized by the perpetrators and greatly feared by the victims.

The next level in this asinine social structure is the defense and law enforcement level. These souls are the soldiers of the despot who are given virtual carte blanche to implement and enforce whatever "laws" or dictates the despot imposes down the line in any manner they desire so long as they are "just following orders". Highly trained to suspect those they are supposed to serve and with access to a wide array of "tools" to "implement" their "initiatives", this level will promote the propaganda that "violence never solves anything" while investing heavily in violence as a deterrent. Religious texts record this level as angels who are messengers of "God" and are created without the ability to choose what initiatives or mandates they follow. Somehow, however, and despite the complete foresight of the despot and the unyielding infallibility of the despot, some of the angels "rebelled" and these angels are called demons. Yes I know this is an oversimplification of the texts but the underlying point remains valid that angels and demons are recorded as the SAME type of being.

This spiritual social structure is, of course, bunk as this is man's best effort to understand the realms of spirit and control the populace. Nothing more... nothing less. The truth of the "structure" of the spiritual realms is much more simple and FAR more benevolent as they are designed to benefit EVERYONE equally. There are helper spirits that exist to assist the growth of each and every soul and they are colloquially known as angels and demons but they are not different souls then what you are. Angels and demons are the same in their intention but are different in their specialization.

Angels can be considered as generalists. Yes there are specializations within the angel phylum but, in general, angels are soft, attractive, and are there to monitor and assist your growth until you no longer need them. Demons, on the other hand, are specialists. Demons are the ones angels deploy when the beneficiary (you) has ignored all other assistance attempts and they need to get you to make a corrective action NOW. When there is an answer to your prayer or an action that you need to take for your growth, your angel will do all they can to get your attention. They may send you signs, whisper in your ear, and softly escalate their methods to get your attention but when you ignore the signs, ignore your dreams, ignore their soft touch, and ignore the brick that was thrown at you... demons are activated.

I realize this statement is oxymoronic and is probably enough to cause the reader some cognitive dissonance as the wisdom presented next runs contra to all your programming and teaching but when the loving demon is activated it is done so as a last resort and its methods are custom tailored to get your attention as quickly as possible. The demon is a loving creature who agrees to use whatever mask or technique necessary to get the attention of the target all the while fully knowing and accepting the fact that whatever is inflicted on to the target will be immediately mirrored and inflicted on to themselves. Their modalities are FAR beyond the soft and gentle energy of the angel but the target is, honestly, ALWAYS in control as the demon will IMMEDIATELY halt its "motivation methodologies" the moment the target either successfully accomplishes the growth opportunity that was the original goal of the angel who deployed the demon or when the target taps in to their truth and respectively commands the demon to stop.

With this understanding and with the knowledge that angels and demons are NOT any different than any other souls allows the reader to understand that the terms spirit guide, guardian angel, angel, and demon are, essentially, interchangeable with the main differentiation being the skill level and level of commitment. As such it is reasonable to consider that a close friend from the past can be a guide that is giving all the love they can to assist your growth. Similarly, in my opinion, ANY being who would knowingly allow themselves to lower their energy and willingly endure whatever they must in order to help you achieve your goal is, undoubtedly, a friend.

Who Cares Analysis	Despite your programming, good and bad are man-made concepts that are deployed in order to divide and concur. By whom and for what purpose is an another book onto itself and is well beyond the scope of this book but it is imperative for the reader to understand that angels and demons are the same being and both "divisions" exist to assist you in your growth. While the actions of the generalist angels tend to be softer and more celebratory in nature, the actions of the specialist demon are NOT evil or "bad"... it is our resistance to the lesson that makes the experience "bad" as we are wholly responsible and completely in control of how long the demon is need for and how much pressure the demon needs to apply.

WHO DO I THINK I AM?

Hopefully the reader has been engaged – or enraged – by the stories I have presented thus far which illustrate that I have some background in darkness and have hinted as to some of the basic tenants of my wisdom but I am sure the reader wants to question me as I have made some grand tales that sound good but the reader wants to pick apart me and my story – as is human nature.

First of all… what is my name? The name the reader will know me by is Singing Hawk. This is a name that was granted to me by the spiritual Council of Elders and it fits me well as I understand it. Essentially, and in a nutshell, the hawk is well known to be the messenger of God and the main weapon of the Angels is song. Similarly the current mantra of many within the paradigm of mainstream religion is that the term universe translates to "one verse" implying song so either way the name Singing Hawk is understood to mean a protected messenger of God which is why I happily embrace it and use it as my name. I also like the Native American connection the name infers and whether or not I have any Native blood in me, in this current incarnation, my past incarnation as a Native American is strong and is commonly found by new readers regardless of their culture or religion.

Those readers who are offended by my association with the Native culture can write whatever letters, emails, or blogs they need to in order to satiate THEIR cultural biases and prejudices because NONE of the readers or Native people I have met with have ANY issue with my association and I have not only worked for Native tribes but I have been FULLY embraced by MANY tribes. The people of the White Mountain Apache Tribe in Pinetop, Arizona, for example, embraced me and my child with open arms when my child and I visited the area to attend a Native American concert. Similarly, while I lived in a mixed community in Sedona, Arizona that included members of Apache, Navajo, and Hopi tribes, my Navajo neighbor mentioned how much he enjoyed visiting my home as the energy was so gentle and clean and while he was Indian… I was Native. I expressed to my Navajo neighbor my concerns with "political correctness" and his retort was that he has full blood relatives that are whiter than me and I should not worry or reduce my wisdom in order to appease ignorance. Sound advice!

Another reason the reader will not know my name beyond my Native name is because I do not want to have to suffer the love of the pious who seek to "convert me" - or more accurately, control me – by physically, mentally, or financially attacking me or my family so that I do not continue to spread my truth which runs contra to their programming. I have experienced the love of the pious in a previous existence and that memory is what has postponed this book that has been pondered and recomposed for some time. Here is what I recall from that experience.

I do not recall the exact timeline but I do recall being the "medicine man" or oracle in a beautiful mountain village. I can still see the green grass, the meadow flowers, and the body of water that was not far from the gentle green hills that surrounded the village. Life was good and I happily and openly embraced my skills and gave freely to all in need. Everyone was happy and prosperous until the dark ones arrived. The dark ones demanded the destruction of everyone and everything that went against their dogmatic control mechanisms and the villagers quickly gave me to the dark ones in a vain, and sadly ineffective, effort to protect themselves. The dark ones took me a place of unimaginable horror and did vile, torturous things to me in order to make me see the "unconditional love" of their "God" and accept their insane "teachings" without question.

While I understand that circumstances and control mechanisms are not the same way contemporary society – or, honestly, we are programmed to NOT say so... such underpinnings remain and are well known. Case in point, no one will bat an eye or debate that the news regularly reports on the fate of some poor soul who defies the "love" of their local religion that is deploying the same thought processes and techniques that their theological cousins used to gain their power and implement their control mechanisms. So if you know me and my non-Native name then good but it is FAR better that the reader does NOT.

Next, why should you listen to me? People are programmed to respect and value the word of "authority" above all others so most tend to listen only to those who have letters behind their name which, most notably, include Ph. D. and MD. . Non-mainstream professional titles like DO and ND are routinely programmed to be ignored or discredited but that is for another essay. Many of my Ph. D. colleagues, friends, and clients, however, commonly discredit themselves by referring to their professional title as "Piled Higher and Deeper" opposed to the commonly accepted philosophiae doctor or doctor philosophiae. While I, admittedly, do not have those credentials available for my curriculum vitae, I have been in doctorate programs but have left for reasons that mainly involve my inability to see long term financial solvency in the career path so my degrees and continuing education are in data science, business management, healing, and spiritual counseling. The reader may find my collection of studies contradictory but they all fit me well.

Among all other things... I am an analyst. I always have been and I always will be. I am the FIRST person to be skeptical of anything outside of the understood and accepted norm which is why I seek to understand whatever I do not know but reviewing all realms possible. I LOVE "forbidden" knowledge as that which is "forbidden" is typically deemed so by some "authority" that is typically trying to hide something in order to promote it's own version but, in many cases, that which is forbidden is the truth needed to make the relevant connection for understanding and assimilation. It is due to and through my study of "phenomena x" that I built my meticulous attention to detail, communication skills, and information technology repertoire that allowed me to excel in information technology, business management, and counseling.

That said, however, I also have umpteen certifications and attunements in a multitude of healing modalities, spiritual counseling methodologies, and disincarnate assistance. I have been a Chaplain for the Unity of Sedona, helped lost and confused souls cross over in to the light, and counseled with darkened souls to learn forgiveness and acceptance during or immediately after some of the worst times in their incarnate or disincarnate lives.

Despite all the education, certifications, and methodologies, however, my main source of information is channeled either at the moment of need or in an "official" Akashic Records reading session. The difference between the two information channel timings is indistinguishable to me as both sources are very closely related and the information received is interchangeable. The just-in-time channeling effect of the at the moment of need, however, is my most common relay methodology and is what steered me away from "mainstream" counseling. Mainstream counseling is very a highly regulated modality whose focus tends to be "disease management" (otherwise known as additional billable hours) whereas the information I receive, when counseling, is laser focused and is exactly what the person needs to know, at that immediate point of time, which typically hits the person square in the heart so I can get to the root cause of an issue and offer a channeled solution that could, otherwise, take many years of sessions of mainstream counseling. Additionally, and honestly, I was not received well as a mainstream counselor as I was said to be not compassionate but nothing could be further from the truth.

I obtained my first degree in Human Services as I was driven by my desire to serve mankind and was searching for the best fit for me. I took whatever course that was available in "professional" healing and wound up with certifications and licensees in Emergency Medicine and counseling. Having overcome addiction and noting the rampant use of self medication and the detrimental challenges typically spawned by such use, I decided to work as a substance abuse counselor while continuing my para-professional study... it did not work out well as I, to my horror, learned that many, if not ALL, of the addicts were not there for help rather they were there to dwell in their misery and find someone to justify their decisions and sorrow by telling them that current circumstances and failures are not their fault. This victim mindset does NOT mesh well with my straight forward style that focuses on self responsibility, acceptance, and forgiveness and I was branded as not compassionate as I refused to tell them that their addiction, bad choices, and low mentality was not their choice or within their control... both are. I did not fall for the common appeal to emotion tripe that I don't have this disease so I don't know how it feels to which I would let the addict know that I was CONCEIVED on drugs and was born suffering from withdrawal so if ANYONE has the right to whine about not having a choice it would be ME. I showed no interest in comparing scars or presenting my self medication resume to them opting to note that I did in fact have the same "disease" despite my choice to NOT use and to face "reality" head on. It soon became apparent to me that I was not able to or interested in working with people who are not seeking or interested in finding help.

So, why should you listen to me? Simply and honestly stated... you shouldn't as I am not your leader, guru, master or ANY related term and I have no intention or desire to be such. I well understand that we are all one energy and that all of us teach and learn from the other. I openly warn and advise ALL people to raise a red flag any time any one says, implies, or conveys that they are "better" than you or "more advanced" then you as this is the basis of a master/slave relationship that is fear and control based. So, rather than listen to me, simply read the message

I am presenting and see how it resonates with your understanding or need and allow whatever wisdom or insight presented to outline to you that I have come from similar circumstances and these are the tools and methodologies I deployed in order to progress along my path. Keep what works and dispose of what does not.

Who Cares Analysis	Who cares who I am? My name and "educational credentials" concerning spiritual topics is truly of no value but I understand that the reader is programmed to value such items so my repertoire was summarized in this section. I can already hear the backlash from people who insist they are not programmed and I am out of my mind… perhaps but consider this proof of programming. Not long ago it was "common knowledge" that there is "absolutely no scientific proof" that cigarette smoking was – in any way – linked to cancer. This was the allowed and protected banter until the truth was allowed to come out and then everyone was programmed to state how evil the tobacco companies are. Well the same "no scientific proof that x causes y" banter remains in wide use to this day and is deployed to dismiss culpability, liability, and responsibility for all kinds of maladies but, honestly, only someone who is programmed could allow the already proven false dogma to exist and follow it completely. For the record, anecdotal evidence IS evidence but YOUR anecdotal evidence means nothing to the establishment and the dogmatic mantra will remain as is and without any deviance until some "authority" tells you otherwise. Yes… you are programmed.

THE SPIRITUAL TIME CLOCK

In my work with darkened and "lost" souls – souls who came to experience some of the same growth challenges I have – it is all too common to see lackluster eyes and hear familiar mantras of defeat and self loathing. I truly LOVE seeing the rekindling of hope in their eyes when I explain the basics of the Spiritual Time Clock as it lets the person know that their journey through darkness is on their path and the darker the current circumstances, the closer they are to the end of the lesson.

In foster care, for example, the depression of the unadopted or those who continually recycle in the system is palatable as despite the foster kid's best effort at "keeping a stiff upper lip" in order to "put their best foot forward", they are well aware of their dismal socioeconomic "status" - or lack thereof – and extreme poverty with dismal opportunities to better themselves. Unadopted foster kids, in fact and sadly, do NOT have, or have access to, any of the luxuries or basic necessities that most other kids take for granted.

Consider, for example, the popular Facebook meme in which a child is bawling about not getting the version of an Apple iPad she wanted having, instead, to suffer the indignity of a lessor model. In this scenario, it is likely (and hopeful) that the child in the meme was sent to her room after her tantrum… a room that most certainly is fully equipped with a comfortable bed, TV, video game system, computer, wireless internet,

etc. whereas the foster kid who simply disagrees with a social or shelter worker runs the risk of GOING TO JAIL. No soft bed, no TV, no computer, no iPad, nothing… nothing but a cold and solitary cell surrounded by similarly angry, lost, and frustrated souls. While the parents of the previous child will surely forgive any and all transgressions caused by the ludicrous tantrum and support the child's future endeavors, the unadopted foster child is not afforded the same forgiveness as they do not have a family to love or protect them. This lack of parental guidance results with many foster children being keenly aware that they are disposable and at the bottom rung of society inflicting deep emotional scars – professionally called structural strain – that lead many females in to "careers" in adult "entertainment" and males in to more aggressive and felonious venues.

No this scenario is NOT the only possible outcome and I am NOT implying ANY version of that statement as I, myself, am a living example of choice over the dogma of nature versus nurture as in both nature and nurture… my statistically expected life path was not good. I, in fact, have a TON of statistical data and psychobabble to support the fact that my nurtured malfeasance is a byproduct of my genetically encoded predispositional inability (nature) to conform to societal norms but I made the deviant and borderline oppositional defiant disorder (psychobabble) CHOICE to not prove my naysayers right. Yes, I have a LOT of REALLY good reasons to fail but I failed to accept that role and I took responsibility for my actions and thoughts and made the changes needed to remove myself from the high probability of incarceration that is the likely outcome for MANY unadopted foster kids who age out of the system.

In fact, and sadly, despite my best efforts and intentions to assist my foster brothers and sisters from following this well beaten path... I am the only one who does not have any of the predicted ailments including addiction, incarceration, homelessness, or any of the other spiritual, psychological, or financial limitations that come with extreme lack. For the record... I tired my best to help detour them but there was only so much I could do as I was in the same financial constraints and came from the same sociopolitical gutter and had to heal from the same mental prison of lack. My savior complex suffered greatly in seeing what I perceived as my failure to help my foster brothers and sisters overcome their challenges but my constant speeches and optimistic encouragement did plant the seeds they need for their success when they are ready to follow and I was able to hear better than expected outcomes for many; albeit, at their funerals.

One of the lessons I present to those who are young and have accepted a great deal of growth challenges is I remind them that you never able to pursue the mastery of more challenges then you have the capacity to successfully overcome so CONGRATULATIONS are in order as your volume of challenges means you are a spiritual badass and are in an advanced class. Such reminder is typically met with a bevy of mixed emotions as this may be the first time in the young one's life in which they hear – or accept – a message of encouragement and love opposed

to hearing the standard – and oftentimes internalized – banter of being a screw up, a loser, having no future, and being worthless. This is as nice and as professional as I can present these limiting phrases as the reader is likely to have heard – or said – something similar that is said with FAR more colorful metaphors and in a far harsher tone.

I recall one foster brother whom I really did not know well because he was young and beginning his cycle of housing assignments when I was close to aging out of the system but I grew weary of his game of throwing his feces at people and I disciplined him. His reaction was to stop throwing his feces at people at least for the remaining time I had in the system and then time went on and almost all of us lost touch. Several years later I was working as a Behavioral Health Technician in a private psychiatric hospital when the system began buzzing about a big black guy who just came in the hospital who has sworn to hurt anyone who looks at him. I was coming on shift and noticed a person setting themselves up in the seclusion room which was a VERY odd occurrence as this is where people usually tried to stay out of. Details of the occurrence are sketchy but what matters is that at some point I went to the water fountain and found myself eye to eye with this person and it was the foster brother that I had disciplined all those years ago! Our reconnection was wonderful and we hugged like the lost brothers we were. Our banter was as lively and full of "colorful metaphors" and everyone was in shock. We reminisced about the lost years and I began to apologize for my disciplinary actions all those years ago. He stopped my apology saying that I really helped him and he always wished to see me again so that he could thank me. I was confused by this and he said that when I disciplined him for his actions, I told him that he was better than this and he needed to stop this nonsense. That was the first time in his life, he said, that someone treated him like a person instead of telling him him that he was a stupid, worthless "offensive racial slur" and it helped him more than I would ever know. I said I was sorry it doesn't seem like it did enough to which he replied... imagine where I'd be without it.

Regardless of age, or challenge load, I introduce the spiritual time clock to the person as the spiritual time clock is a tool I have been introducing to people since I was able to speak and it helps people understand the natural flow of "awakening" and I have used it to rekindle the light in those who are darkened and feel lost as I can show them that their journey through the darkness brings them closer to enlightenment and unity.

For me, the Spiritual Time Clock has always been a source of encouragement and joy... not just because of the wonderful messages it portrays but also because it is a path to Nerdvana

(a humorous euphemism for nerd Heaven) for me when I realized how wonderfully the Spiritual Time Clock matches the Cartesian Plane. I surely just triggered some readers in to an Algebraic panic as they NEVER expected to hear an Algebraic concept in a spiritual book! Calm down and rest assured that I will not be presenting any formulae or ask you to solve any problems so there is no need to raise your mathphobe defenses. For those who are ready to move beyond their math induced shock, let me remind you what the Cartesian Plane is so you can understand how the Spiritual Time Clock is in alignment.

In a nutshell, and for the purposes of this book, the Cartesian Plane is simply your standard graph in which the user plots two coordinates, x (horizontal) and y (vertical). The plotting of points and curves is not relevant in this discussion but what does matter is that the intersection of the x and y coordinates creates four quadrants that are commonly defined as:

- Quadrant 1 = +,+
- Quadrant 2 = +,-
- Quadrant 3 = -,-
- Quadrant 4 = -,+

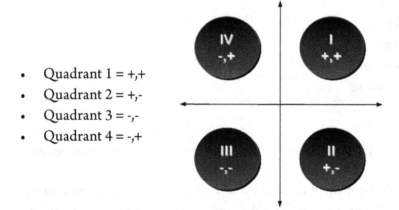

To aid the recollection of the reader, the coordinates corresponding to the quadrants are read as x,y so Quadrant 1 indicates that the value of x is positive and the value of y is positive. Put your mind at ease as it does not matter what the value of x or y is so long as they are both positive (greater than 0) values. Similarly each quadrant

can be extrapolated accordingly so the value of x, in quadrant 4, is negative (less than 0) and the value of y is positive. For the nerds getting bent out of shape that I am defining the terms positive and negative in relation to 0 without defining 0... it's OK. The idea presented herein is to designed to be as simple and easy as possible so you are welcome to comment on this to your heart's content but it will not change the simplicity I am purposely conveying.

Now overlay an analog time clock within the Cartesian Plane and you get the Spiritual Time Clock whose clockwise flow amazing and PERFECTLY matches a generalized road map of the consciousness of the reader. At this point I have to admit something… I have PURPOSELY spent my experience REFUSING to document this because controlling forces LOVE to control any and all information that is – in any way – a perceived threat to its programming and control mechanisms by having its agents issue a social control to program the populace to dismiss it or to allow the concept be reduced to the ridiculous by saturating the market with umpteen versions of it so the populace is confused and does not comprehend the underlying message and value of the tool. For those considering this fact to be a three letter government agency coined term to prevent the populace from thinking independently (known as a conspiracy theory), consider what most people think about ancient oracle tools like astrology, the runes, the i-ching, and other similar tools. Next contrast that with what happened to the words of previous guides who gave freely and implored their students to NOT follow them… teachings of freedom, unconditional love, and truth became religions with STRICT dogma that disallows any thought or action outside of its agreed upon contemporaneous definition and confines of "morality". Noting this, it is my sincere hope that the populace has evolved to a point that they can use this tool as a tool and NOT allow a tool to become dogma or "a parlor trick".

The overlay allows the Spiritual Time Clock to have four quadrants with three sections within each quadrant. This amends the quadrant list, presented previously, as:

Quadrant 1

Coordinates: +,+
Time: 0 – 3 o'clock
Season: Summer
Wisdom Stage: Infant, Toddler
Analogies: Beginning

Common Phrase(s)
Live "In the Light", "Stay Positive", "I'm such a good person"

This is the beginning of the cycle and is where most are. People are well intended and tend to follow authority without question as authority is safe and freedom is found in obeying rules. Many of those who are within the 1 and 2 range are living their lives within the confides of religion while those who are closer to 3 claim to be freethinkers and deploy deviant and happy titles like lightworker, hippy, or social justice warrior. Typically those in this quadrant find life to be a constant party and all that matters is image, wealth, and personal comfort. There is a lot of competition in this quadrant for status and these souls can be very selfish, highly judgmental, and extremely manipulative while loudly touting their self righteousness and love for all who think, act, and speak like them. The focus of this quadrant is to stay in the light and always be positive which, paradoxically, is highly imbalanced as many chose to remain in this quadrant due, in part, to their fear of moving forward – i.e. fear of the dark – and cannot see that their fear based lack of movement essentially renders them a prisoner of the light.

Quadrant 2

Coordinates: +,-
Time: 4 – 6 o'clock
Season: Fall
Wisdom Stage: Child / Teen
Analogies: The Descent, Loss of Comfort, Loss of Ego, Nothing is as it was

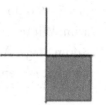

Common Phrase(s)
"Why Me?", "It's too hard", "There is no hope", "My life is Hell"

For many, this quadrant is akin to jumping out of a plane with a parachute that does not open only to find the rapidly approaching ground is guarded by trees of rusty razors that ends in a lake of fiery acid… it is not pretty and it, literally, can be Hell on Earth. Many find that they are ill prepared for the challenges that manifest to embrace them when they find the courage to move forward from the first quadrant. Things were pretty good while the soul hovered around the 3 mark but the closer they get to the 6 mark… the worse life becomes. Nothing is the same as it was and many turn to whatever they can find to find a temporary reprieve from the never-ending, yet rapidly increasing, onslaught of life challenges. Many of these souls become completely frustrated, wholly disillusioned, and are unable to see any way out as they trap themselves in addiction, violence, and extreme mental duress only to "awake" one day and find they are without friends or family. Many do not pass this quadrant and turn to suicide for a way out. The paradox here is that these souls cannot see that their movement from the safety and surety of the light has afforded them more wisdom and accomplishment then they could ever have experienced in the first quadrant. Honestly, and unfortunately for those nearing the 6 mark, this truth is of little consolation as, no matter how well the message was received, all the soul can see is inconceivable darkness that is without any light at the end of the tunnel.

The end of second quadrant (point 6 on the Spiritual Time Clock) is the dreaded, but blessed, dark night of the soul. At this time in the Spiritual Time Clock life indeed is Hell and the soul finds that they are at TRUE rock bottom… the lowest possible point of their life. Addictions and ALL other techniques that used to bring even the most minute of refuge no longer eases the pain or affords any pleasure. Life is a constant nightmare that the soul cannot awaken from as the world seems endlessly dark and is void of any joy or pleasure. Everyone and everything seems out to get you and you are incapable of doing anything right. There are LOTS of suicides, homicides, and psychotic breaks in or around this point and the soul is completely broken and left to find and rebuild itself. The paradox here is that this IS the answer to most people's prayers as it is in this dark place that a soul is freed from their programming and ego and have the capacity to find their truth and reconnect. This is sacred time of rebirthing and while the birthing pains can be intense and extended… those who emerge from their compressed carbon based manure cocoon find themselves fully restored as an immeasurably brilliant and flawless diamond with an innate understanding of love and themselves.

Quadrant 3

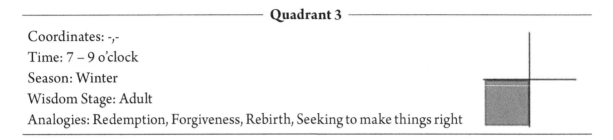

Coordinates: -,-
Time: 7 – 9 o'clock
Season: Winter
Wisdom Stage: Adult
Analogies: Redemption, Forgiveness, Rebirth, Seeking to make things right

---

Common Phrase(s)
"If only...", "What did I do...", "I can fix...", "Why didn't they listen..."

The unimaginable horrors and challenges of the second quadrant are complete and the soul emerges in to this quadrant with renewed zest and the desire to help everyone achieve the same love and understanding they found and have. Prejudices, fear, hate, competition, and negativity dissipate and the well intended, and recently reborn, soul is, typically, remorseful for the mistakes it perceives it made during its journey so it vows to save as many other souls as possible from taking a similar path not realizing that it was the "mistakes" (or growth challenges) that brought the soul to its current wisdom. The paradox here is the healed soul who has dedicated its life to the service and well-being of others can become extremely frustrated and hurt by those who it seeks to serve when it learns those souls may not ready to move forward regardless of the amount of heartrending noise made by the soul-in-need, the position of the soul-in-need on the Spiritual Time Clock, or the best effort of the quadrant 3 soul. This painful "Savor Complex" can slow the progression of the quadrant 3 soul and mirrors why this quadrant is double negative on the Cartesian Plane (-,-)... broken hearts, frustrations, and disappointments are rampant for the quadrant 3 soul.

Quadrant 4

Coordinates: -,+
Time: 10 – 12 o'clock
Season: Spring
Wisdom Stage: Elderly
Analogies: Balance, Humor, Unity, Acceptance

Common Phrase(s)
"All is as it should be", "In their own time...", "Planting seeds..."

Balance is achieved and the limitations of "duality" are understood and unified. Life becomes less of a struggle and more of a good laugh. Tunnel vision that what previously laser focused on the micro level gives way to a wide angle lens of the macrocosm. The perfect perfection of imperfection is celebrated and each individual is loved for its expression of its authentic uniqueness. A healthy detachment brings the quadrant 4 soul closer than ever as seeds are planted and encouraged to grow.

Unconditional love. The blessings of light and dark are revealed and love permeates and flows freely from everywhere and everything. Life becomes a divine comedy and egotistical pursuits give way to universal harmony. Life is multidimensional and all are one.

These summaries are wide encompassing but still clearly outline an approximation of the soul's growth. It should be noted, however, that this is just an approximation of one's position on the Spiritual Time Clock and does not necessarily relay or constitute the person's overall growth. I implore the reader to NOT use this tool in an effort or exercise to determine irrelevant and categorical controls such as higher or lower, better or worse, or more or less advanced as each person can go through SEVERAL cycles in a lifetime. Please recall that those who are gifted with the heaviest burdens and challenge load are true ambassadors of love regardless of their immediate position on the Spiritual Time Clock as, once again, you cannot take on more of a challenge load than you are able to successfully overcome. So rather then use this tool as another tool to categorize and judge people use this tool as it is intended and presented… to see that those who are in the darkness are truly courageous beings

So rather than look at kids and teenagers who hit their 6 LONG before you can fathom it as bad, worthless, and scum… try thanking them for the lessons they are bringing for your growth and theirs.

Yes people can do dumb things and make VERY bad decisions but whatever the circumstances, this is for growth… yours and theirs. Unfortunately, many can get stuck at a certain point for some time but those who are struggling are, generally, further along than those who are not.

Who Cares Analysis	My hesitant introduction of the Spiritual Time Clock is done for two main, but intertwined, purposes: (1) to let people know they are not as bad as they think they are and (2) to let people know they are not as good as they think they are. The projected mask of an angel or a devil are simply illusions as we ALL are, paradoxically, both and neither as good and bad are simply arbitrary judgments that are based on the norms of any given society at a fixed point of time. This tool is meant to be a guide and NOT a dogmatically followed religion with detailed accuracy. I am sure there will be someone who comes out of the woodwork with some revisioning of this and who is attempting to profit from this new, advanced version but do NOT listen to such tripe and use this guide to find the hope you need when you are stuck.

WHAT DO I KNOW ABOUT JESUS CHRIST?

Religion is a topic I did not want to touch upon formally in this book but the message popped in to my head and I know I will not get ANY sleep until I compose this so here we go!

First and foremost, despite my research in to "forbidden" knowledge, mythology, and world regions, my personal knowledgebase and experience is from a western perspective and more aptly, Christian perspective. My knowledgebase of the Christian theology is derived from personal study, theological programming, and channeling. When I was under the influence of Christianity I actively participated in the business of "saving" souls, helped friends through seminary, and assisted new Theologians begin their tax exempt career. That said, however, I, like the mythical teacher known as Jesus, am anti-religion but I see some value in the implementation of the structure and hope a soul can find in their initial acceptance of religion.

Personally I am fine if the previous paragraph makes you want to burn this book as you have to purchase the book before you can burn it so tell ALL your friends and burn them all! For those, however, who are better composed and able to consider information that triggers your cognitive dissonance without the thoughts of or desire to teach me about the peaceful and loving teachings of Jesus through violence, threats, or other church sponsored "motivation" techniques… let me explain.

There is VERY little evidence for the existence of the being called Jesus Christ and the lack of such evidence is already very well documented so I will not bore the reader with the details save one irrefutable point… there was never ANYONE born with the name of Jesus Christ (at least not in the time period the character in question is supposed to have existed) as the term Christ is a TITLE… NOT a name. Similarly, much, if not most, of the data attributed to this character are apparent plagiarisms compiled from other mythologies that existed at the time of the "appearance" of this character. A reasonable person is prudent to question why someone who was supposedly so controversial has NO contemporary writings as everyone who is alleged to have any knowledge of the character waited decades or centuries after the death of the character to record their knowledge. In this day and age the "news" bombards the populace with every trivial element of some "celebrity's" life in real-time and without pause so it is odd that there has not been ANY discovery of anything concerning ANYTHING this character is alleged of doing during the time period of his "life".

With that said, I have a disclosure to make… I have met that character in channelings and in healings so while I cannot confirm that the character portrayed in the Bible existed, I personally know the image of the embodiment of the "Christ Consciousness", and, according to my grandmother, am genetically related to it.

My grandmother was one for embellishments so I really did not give much credence to many of the stories she would tell. I recall sometime in the 80's when she made the off comment that we are the bloodline of Jesus and that she had seen Jesus in our house. At that time I was to angry to care and I did not think about it again until the 90's when a major movie was released with the plot being highly reminiscent of what she had claimed a decade or so previously. Again, my grandmother was prone to embellishment so before you get your panties in a bunch and demand proof of – or blood for – my blasphemous statement note a few things... (1) I do not know if this statement is true and do NOT make any warrants or claims to its authenticity as I present it here for trivia's sake, (2) I now, as then, do NOT care if my grandmother's unverifiable allegation is true, and (3) you, the reader, have NO way of knowing if this statement is in any way true so relax and focus on the MESSAGE I am trying to convey. With that and to further inflame the reader... my grandmother even gave me a picture!

I do not recall when I received this pic and I cannot prove that this picture is in any way authentic but the note that accompanied the pic implied this picture was taken in the late 1800's and the image contained therein was taken without an intended subject. I do not know where my grandmother obtained the photo and I have not been able to find a copy of it on Google despite whatever search I try so I am unable to present the purported image of a person that I cannot verify ever existed physically due to, reasonable and fair, potential copyright concerns. I am sure the curious, but disappointed, reader understands and forgives this unverifiable omission.

MY EXPERIENCES WITH THIS BEING

I have met this being on at least three occasions that I can recall.

The first meeting came shortly after I accepted religious dogma and began to dim my light in order to fit in. I was surprised to find myself in a personal meeting with the namesake of the religion and did not feel worthy to be there. I was equally bewildered and confused when Jesus told me that I was beyond this and not to follow the programming of the religion.

Another meeting happened within the same relative timeframe as I again found myself in front of Jesus but I had not adhered to his advice as religious life – despite its prejudices, controlling nature, and strict control – appealed to me. I found a place where I seemed to be accepted and the more I assimilated in to the culture, the more attractive I began to appear to the females in the congregation. During this meeting, I confess, that I did not hear a single word of the conversation because I was fixated on what was behind Jesus... a chasm filled with Hellfire. I do not recall how long Jesus continued before he stopped, looked at me, and asked me if I was alright. I was completely overtaken by fear and the ONLY thing I could think to do was to ask if that was were I was going. Jesus seemed surprised and inquired if I was concerned by the Hellfire behind him.

I found myself shaking with fear but denied what was plainly obvious. A smile crossed his lips and the Hellfire immediately became Heaven Light at which time I awoke grateful for seeing what is to come but disappointed and somewhat ashamed that I had not heard anything that Jesus came to share. I found I had allowed myself to be programmed with fear so that I was unable to receive a message of love from a master.

My next meeting occurred at an event I attempted to avoid. I had cast aside the shackles of religion and was looking to heal the root causes of my issues that originally addicted me to religion. I had met a psychic in the Atlanta area and was surprised as this was the first psychic I was unable to debunk (using my own gifts) so I decided to partake in a program that was supposed to help me find balance. The day of the healing came and I decided that I was NOT going to go and I was going to bury myself in work to manifest a reasonable excuse as to why I did not go and why I was unable to call to cancel the appointment... it did not work. Shortly after settling the plan in my mind, I was called to the Director's office and laid off effective immediately. In a state of mild shock and bewilderment, I gathered my things and left the office and drove away. Now, I thought, that my cash flow had suddenly dried up I definitely was NOT going to go as I needed the cash for my family's bills. To my amazement and despite the fact that I purposely drove in a path that was OPPOSITE of the meeting area, I found that I had arrived in the meeting area at the RIGHT time! To this day I still do not understand or am able to explain how I got there as the sheer volume of traffic would have normally prevented my arrival but here I was. I contemplated continuing on my path but a thought came to me that made me consider the impossibility and improbability of me being here yet here I was despite all my plans and efforts otherwise so I decided to surrender and I pulled in to the meeting area.

The healing session started with me still trying to find any way I could to not attend but as soon as I would think of an objection the psychic would verbalize an answer or take corrective action which effectively rendered my creative excuse repertoire useless. The psychic then sounded surprised and told me that the spirit in attendance for me and who would be facilitating my healing was the Christ energy who wanted to be identified to ensure I realized who it was that made sure I attended the session and how special I really am. At that moment all of the implausible events I had encountered throughout the day suddenly made sense as I realized that all of the irrational and impossible events that occurred were done to counter my shenanigans and get me to this healing session. It was also relayed that the Christ energy has EVERYTHING under control so I can relax, accept the healing gift, and not worry about the job, money, or anything else… everything I could find to worry about was already taken care of. It sounded good but I still maintained a healthy "skepticism" concerning the authenticity of the psychic's words until I closed my eyes.

The moment I closed my eyes I found the expected darkness was brighter than the day outside. I suspected the psychic was trying to pull a fast one and opened my eyes only to find the same darkened room and the psychic still in a couch on the other side of the room. The brightness was still there when I closed my eyes again so I relaxed and basked in this bright spiritual light. I was content to spend the entire session basking in this light but I was in for a surprise as close to the end of the process I experienced something that I will never forget but struggle to put into words.

I became aware of the Christ energy surrounding me… embracing me. I found the immensely gentle and loving energy began to "cleanse" my body and mind of the negativity I guarded inside. I became aware of the spirit entering my body as I felt a wonderful cool and soft energy first in my toes and soon in my legs. I was bewildered at the softness of this experience and truly in awe as I found my body in the most wonderful state of perfect coolness that matched my innately preferred temperature wherever the spirit had been. I knew, instinctively, that I was in complete control and the spirit would leave the instant I demanded should I feel any fear or not be comfortable yet I was so at peace with these feelings that I found it humorous to feel the spirit making physical adjustments to my posture to aid its journey. At one point, even though I am completely aware of this being impossible physically, I felt as if my body was floating above the chair. I continued to be in awe of this experience as it worked its way through my body and out through my skull. The end result was amazing and I happily paid the psychic and offered my sincere gratitude for having the session.

| Who Cares Analysis | The being colloquially known as Jesus Christ would be appalled at what those who use its namesake do... not just to others who do not follow those who claim its namesake but in general. Of course there is a LOT of missing text pertaining to this being so much of what I state is from my personal understanding of and meetings with this being. This being CLEARLY states we are all one and ALL are equal but you have allowed those who have other "goals" in mind to program you otherwise... to your detriment and to their betterment. Look within – without bias – and find the "Kingdom of Heaven" therein. To find the true light, however, you need to have the courage to enter the dark. |

WHAT IS MY OPINION ON RELIGION?

As mentioned previously, for the most part, I am anti-religion. In fact, here is an example of my writing on religion taken from a prototype of this book:

[Religion is nothing more than man's pre-Machiavellian tripe "granting" man the "divine authorization" to do whatever the hell he pleases. A quick summary of Machiavelli's "The Prince" is you are the prince and therefore it is your right to do whatever to hell you please to whomever stands in your way. Likewise, the God of Religion is a manmade deity created to grant man freedom and "moral justification" to rape, kill, slaughter, and enslave whatever stands in the way of short-term egotistical gains. In other words, the God of Religion is a manmade scapegoat granting man freedom from his conscience... nothing more, nothing less.

Some people, however, have learned to harness the power of religion for personal gain, political power, and to generate fear in those who prefer to be led. These Disinformation Agents (DA's) will preach that only through their leadership or understanding of the "sacred texts" can a person find salvation. Do NOT let these DA's mislead you and steal your power and hard earned wealth. These people do not have your best interests at heart and are actively masking their intentions to gain your trust. Once they have successfully gained access to your spiritual and financial reserves, the DA will immediately employ tactics to maintain your obedience while raping you financially and spiritually.]

My understanding of religion has grown since I initially inscribed those words and gone further on my own path on the Spiritual Time Clock so I have grown to understand that religion, like demons, has a role to play in the growth of the soul regardless if the interaction is "good" or "bad".

I will begin this section by outlining some of the bad things about religion so that the reader has something to look forward to, although, there will be quite a few who agree with the following observations. The horrors of the "faithful" are well documented in history despite the current incarnation's attempt to whitewashing everything they prefer not to discuss. There is a GOOD reason why the period in which the Church was law is known as the "Dark Ages". The church demands its congregants have zealous and unwavering commitment to whatever they say without holding the "leadership" to the same requirements. The ludicrous origin story of "original sin", for example, is completely invalidated by the church protectors who seek to sidestep any responsibility and all liability of their long history of rape, abuse, and terror by stating they are not responsible for the mistakes of the past while still attempting to sell the "fall" of mankind occurred when a person

– that all living people throughout history is alleged to be a descended from – took a bite of an apple that was offered by a talking snake. I can buy the talking snake part – as I also have talked with snakes – but stating that ALL of mankind is inescapably condemned to pain, suffering, and eternal damnation due to the alleged misdeed of a mythological woman while claiming no responsibility for the MUCH more vile and heinous actions in a contemporaneous administrative culture is more of a fairy tale that I can swallow… and I LOVE fairy tales and animated adventures!

Yes, you read that correctly, I have talked with snakes and here is an example. I was an external hire for a family business in Florida. The family was from Kentucky and they were working a virtual gold mine in the property preservation business as there was plenty of work and all the clients paid well and on time. Everyone in the family was really a decent person who worked hard, was friendly, and liked to get loud when they played. One day it happened that a snake came in to the home office and its accidental arrival was observed by one of the female family members who began screaming thereby working all the male family members in to a frenzy. They where hooting and hollering and began scurrying around looking for their guns and a wastebasket. As an empath and a healer who had talked to snakes before this incident, I knew I had to do what I could to save the snake's life but I did not want to expose my "native" talents as these people were pretty religious and not too understanding of alternative techniques. I waited until everyone was preoccupied with whatever they were doing and I went to the snake. As is commonly the case, the young snake was terrified as it did not know where it was, did not like the air conditioning on its skin, and could feel the sheer volume of energy its arrival caused and its

terror was palatable as the energy surrounding it was extremely jittery and uneven. I quickly smoothed the snake's energy so that it would listen and not run away (this would, most likely, have sealed its fate) and said to it that I knew it was scared and did not mean any harm but these people are scared as well and are looking to defend their home and family. I let it know the best thing it could do was to turn around and go back out the door. The snake stopped, looked at me, and did exactly as I asked much to the disappointment of the male family members who arrived shortly thereafter. In my focus on the snake, however, I did NOT keep my energy wide so I did not see the family matriarch there until I turned around. Her mouth was agape and I was not sure what to say or how to react but I did not have to wait long as when the males arrived and asked where the snake was she simply stated that I told the snake to leave and it did. The looks I got from the males was an odd mixture of disbelief, disappoint, and wonder.

The fun part of this story is the church would have "rewarded" my loving and life saving actions by doing terrible things to me had I been found out not that long ago. There are still factions that remain in existence, that are not solely Christian, who would LOVE to do such things because I am doing things that they reserve exclusively for their deities – even though we ALL have the ability. Indeed, religions, as a whole, has taken the loving words, enlightened actions, and unconditional acceptance that was offered and demonstrated by a few masters and converted such blessings in to a strict, dogmatic nightmare whose teachings and "promotion" is the bane of those who they claim to emulate.

Admittedly and candidly this section is a struggle for me. I have spent entire experiences fighting against the enslaving confide that is religion so for me to find any value in it shows I have, finally, overcome my Savior Complex.

Now the first good point I have for religion agrees, in part, with the Marxian observation that religion is "the opiate of the masses" as religion does, in fact, allow the constituent a reprieve from "normalcy" which can be addictive. No I am not a student or adept of Marx and I do not follow the philosophy he relayed any more or any less than I am a student or adept of the philosophy of Jesus, Buddha, or Hitler. I remind the reader who is clawing their eyes out at my inconceivable audacity of naming the reprehensible name of Hitler in the same sentence as Jesus, that balance is negative positive so to be balanced one must transcend dark and light by embracing, understanding, and transforming the two sides of the same whole in to one in their mind. Pursuant to this, and as an admitted student of "forbidden" knowledge, wisdom is obtained by knowing ALL sides and by knowing ALL sides, the adept is FAR better at seeing through the smoke and mirrors of society and making a big picture decision then those who are imbalanced. Similarly I am NOT a student of history in the manner of "professional" and "educated" historians who derive great pleasure in knowing every inane and mundane detail of subject x. Personally, I do NOT care that subject x went to the bathroom at this time and on this date and then did y. No, that level of trivial detail is of NO importance to me BUT I DO value the lessons and quotes of subject x and will pay attention to those items in order to gain the wisdom that subject x is inscribed to impart.

Another benefit is that social structure can be temporarily invalidated as members of different socioeconomic "classes" can meet within the religious landscape which is highly unlikely to occur elsewhere. Yes I am well aware that there is a somewhat rigid disparity even within this benefit as it is well documented that certain flavors of religion attract a certain socioeconomic section of the population which, in turn, is the genesis of the taboo phenomenon known as church shopping. Church shopping was born when people learned that a good way to move ahead in social status and at work is to go to the same religious institution as those that are in "higher" positions in your work and is an active strategy that its users admit to in hushed tones.

Another benefit, and in alignment with the previous point of allowing the constituent a temporary reprieve, is that religion gives the seeker a scapegoat as now they have the ability to blame their woes on an invisible judge who cannot be seen or accessed but knows all, sees all, and controls all so they have no responsibility and must live fully to appease this judge. This point is easier to sell as the western mind is typically programmed, at an early age, to accept this paradigm of the fictional, invisible judge that lives in an inaccessible place, watches all kids ALL of the time, knows if they are good or bad, and rewards them accordingly... such is Santa Claus.

The next benefit is something that is completely foreign to me as it is the reason I did not like the confides of religion... complete control. Many people who find their lives lacking whatever it is they perceive as lacking in, find comfort in the rigid, predictable structure of religion as they have lived the life of chaos prior. To me, this oxymoronic, inverted logic is wholly unreasonable but I have seen the benefit of instilling structure in the mind of the chaotic.

I recall a gang member I knew who was notorious for his assaultive behavior and hatred for anyone outside of his dark skin color. He grew up in social services and learned how to get his way through violence early on. I was never able to confirm – or interested in confirming – his claims that he and his gang would purposely drive slow so they could assault anyone who would dare honk at them – especially those of another skin color – and, in one case, he supposedly knocked one person to the ground and then put a motorcycle wheel on top of the defenseless person and peeled out in order to revel in his palatable hate and maximize the pain and fear of his victim! Surprisingly, he and I never really clashed despite both of us being very angry and having met in some very dark places and me having his favorite trigger… a different skin color. He stayed on his path of anger, hate, and violence despite being warned umpteen times that his behavior would eventually be rewarded with incarceration but this was not a deterrent to him as he was very accustomed to dealing with and manipulating government "officials" and had been in LOTS of programs and juvenile detention centers throughout his life. The prediction came true the day he became an adult. I do not recall the charges that punched his ticket to prison but I did not see him for several years later. When our paths crossed again, I was shocked and barely recognized him.

My child and I were shopping at a thrift store when a worker approached me and began to apologize for his past actions. I honestly am not good with faces – as I focus on the energy – so I was having trouble figuring out what this polite and respectable person was talking about until he mentioned a situation we shared and I realized who he was. I was amazed at the difference in his personality and demeanor and he admitted it was prison that helped him find his way. I was overjoyed for his success and we parted as old friends who sincerely and authentically wish the best for the other.

Such is an example of what the instillment of structure can accomplish when implemented and assimilated. Truthfully, religion does not typically enforce the same level of "structure" as the penal colony does but when it does, the implementation is, unfortunately, overdone and leads to darkness which, of course and eventually, finds the light. Thus the final benefit of religion.

Who Cares Analysis	This was a hard section for me to write as I have battled the evils of religion throughout many experiences. Those who are paying attention, however, will be able to look at the Spiritual Time Clock and have an understanding of where I am as I would not have been able to write such a section not too long ago. Darkness, truly is the best illumination for the light!

WHAT ABOUT REINCARNATION?

This will surprise many but I do not believe the concept of reincarnation as it is generally understood in today's culture. People may see my rationalization as a play on words but where some see semantics, I see a logical error.

The traditional definition of the term reincarnation is loosely held as the essence of a deceased person is transferred in to a new body and thus returned to life. This entire concept is prefaced on one main element but the element is something we truly do not experience, death.

Yes I understand that there are umpteen stories about "reincarnation" throughout history and in every culture (even if admitted in hushed tones) and I have openly talked about my past experiences (colloquially known as past lives) but the prudent and attentive reader takes note that I have never talked about death except to outline stories. The reason for this is that death does not occur.

Yes, if you incarnate (in body) then the time will come when you are disincarnate (not in body). Just because you are not in a body does not mean you do not exist or, as many would say, dead. The sheer fact that many recall past experiences and the similarities reported from people who relay their "near death" experience clearly shows that the essence exists without the need for the body.

I can already hear the scoffing of those who are adepts in the religion of science who believe that your existence simply ends when you are no longer in the body and that is fine. I am not here to change your mind and I have no need to sell you on this wisdom as you will find out I am right when the time comes. What is important to understand, however, is that death, in the sense you are programmed to understand and fear, does not exist.

"Death", in truth, is simply the removal of your clothing (your body) and returning to where you came from before you entered your meat puppet; therefore, reincarnation is simply putting on another meat puppet in order to have another experience. Yes, your circumstances will change and you will have to relearn a foreign language and culture in order to function (your native tongue is thought) and succeed in your experience but your essence (or soul) is eternal so you will "change clothes" as many times as you choose. It is through this "costume change" that you can experience all of the variants of existence and experience the challenges and joy of each that is incumbent in the varied role.

Who Cares Analysis	You have been programmed to believe "you only live once" which is, technically a true statement as you never die, but such propaganda exists solely to keep you in fear and under control. Trying to limit and control an unlimited being is impossible so you have to convince the being to internalize this limiting belief in order to implement the belief and control the being.

WHY IS THERE ONE "GOD"?

In short, there's not.

Now for the more fun answer. ALL of us are a part of "God" which, therefore extrapolates in to the inconvenient truth that we are ALL God. Notwithstanding this answer, which is sure to make some lose their minds, even the Bible describes the existence of other "Gods" when "God" states, "You shall have no other Gods before me" or "You must not have any other God but me", depending on the translation you prefer. Regardless of your choice of translation, the quoted verse (Exodus 20:3, New International Version and New Living Translation versions respectively, Exodus 20:3 You shall have no other gods before Me. (2020). Available at: https://biblehub.com/exodus/20-3.htm) "God" refers to Gods which is plural and implies more than one. Dogmatic theologists are quick to take such verses out of context (which they forbid you from doing) and imply that this was "God" referring to the other parts of "itself" and which is taught to embody the father, the son, and the holy spirit. Each of these fractions are supposedly the same being and, allowing credence to the dogmatic viewpoint that each is – essentially – an equal fractal of "God". If that is the "gospel" truth then one is wise to ponder the contradictory construct of why "God" demanded to be first – before another other of the equal fractals of itself...

The concept of a single "God" is one of the most asinine concepts to ever have been perpetuated in to the "consciousness" of mankind and is used solely for the purpose of control. There is a reason why government and religion tend to be innately intertwined... historically, and honestly, religion tends to format the brain of the peasant to accept the rule of the government as is illustrated in the very suspect biblical verse, "... Render to Caesar the things that are Caesar's...". (Mark 12:17 Then Jesus told them, "Give to Caesar what is Caesar's, and to God what is God's." And they marveled at Him. (2020). Available at: https://biblehub.com/mark/12-17.htm). This highly dubious "message" appears to be the work of a governmental interest opposed to the wisdom of a being that is a fractal of the all knowing, all powerful "God" whose knowledge and scope should be WELL beyond the trappings of terrestrial governmental "interests". This low level formatting installs self policing, fear based, viral software in the person which allows the person to justify, rationalize, and engage in the ruthless slaughter, torture, and enslavement of innocent people who believe in other "Gods" as governments know that it is FAR easier to control one mindset than multiple and grant organized religion carte blanche and whole immunity for its "methods" and tendency to "work in mysterious ways".

Who Cares Analysis	There are currently well over an estimated 5,000 different "Gods" being worshiped across the globe. Regardless of the "God" you prefer – including the religion of science – each external "God" tends to be a caricature designed to explain some phenomenon via a thought provoking story making each "God" as valid as they are invalid. The "God(s)" you believe in and give power to exist because of your belief as YOU are a portion of the true God and should appreciate yourself as such.

TO THE MEMBERS OF MY SOUL TRIBE

I know what you feel as I feel the same... we are blessed with exceptional technological and spiritual knowledge but are unable to function financially. Many of us have turned to the abysmal ravages of self medicating or isolation in order to feel normal or accepted but it is time to stop. No matter what form of poison you ingest or how far you isolate yourself, you will never fit in and you should not... you are FAR more advanced which is why you can not fit in.

You came here NOT to participate in the worldly dogmas of greed, selfishness, control, and exclusion but to oppose it by demonstrating love, acceptance, and inclusion – concepts foreign to this plane. As such, you ARE an outsider trying to fit in but you have gone too far as you have begun doubt the very essence of your being in order to fit in. You have allowed the darkness to force you to hide your gifts and even turn you from your innate sacred knowledge. Many of us have unspoken skills that are foreign or "evil" according to the dogma guardians of this realm and do our best to repress these blessings which is the true source of your suffering. STOP NOW!

Feeling the heartbeat of the universe is NOT a sin. Being able to communicate with the elements and nature is NOT a sin. Being one with ALL of existence is NOT a sin. Being blessed with the ability to find scarce resources in the vastness of the mantle is NOT a sin. Being able to see or feel what others can not neither makes you sick nor is it a sin. You must see your unspoken skills as the blessings they are and stop trying to fit in to this backwoods realm so that YOU can benefit from your skills and knowledge opposed to continuing to allow dark soul sucking sycophants to reap the financial rewards of your blessings while enslaving and damning you.

Those who are not members of our Tribe will have no idea what we are talking about – fiction perhaps – but for those who are members... my sentiments will reverberate deep within your soul. STOP trying to fit in to the darkness that you are here to oppose and allow your brilliant light to shine! You take pains to understand and love these people unconditionally – another foreign concept – but it is time for you to look at your own light and grant yourself the same understanding as you give to others freely. You do NOT need to suffer to understand. You do not have to be limited. Be the unconditional love you are and allow yourself to bless everyone, everything, and YOURSELF without any attachment to the BS that permeates this plane.

End your suffering and doubt and you will have accomplished what you came to do.

| **Who Cares Analysis** | This is an old post I composed and is included herein without editing so that the reader can see both my growth since this was inscribed and feel the intention and absorb the medicine of the text. Many needlessly embrace pain in a gross misunderstanding of love and desperately need the love they share. |

HOW CAN YOU FIGHT DARKNESS?

This is a great question as this can be a sticking point for many who valiantly attempt to overcome this challenge. I also know that until you are ready to receive the answer, you will not even recognize the answer or you will not value the answer as you will find the answer to be too simple or unrealistic. So, without further ado, the short answer is: you can't.

Now for the long answer... to wit I am going to make some sweeping and generalized assumptions. First some of the most basic and generalized tenants of the universe include EVERYTHING is love and EVERYTHING happens for your benefit. This knowledge begs the age old question of why bad things happen to good people which is intricately, and redundantly, intertwined with the question of how to fight evil and presents the second assumption... you are not ready to. The simple fact that you are looking to fight darkness revels that you are not aligned with the first statement and are making things FAR more complicated (which is human commonplace) then necessary as this is control mechanism which is derived from fear as opposed to embracing the growth challenge with love.

Yes, I know. The above paragraph is MUCH easier to type than to live and the reader, most likely, feels I am avoiding the question and not providing the answer they want to hear so here is another way of saying the above... violence begets violence so fighting darkness GIVES power to the darkness which I am sure is NOT the intention of the reader so what do you do? Doing nothing is stagnation which does not allow the reader to progress and means the darkness will remain unchanged. Fighting darkness emboldens and strengthens the core issue allowing the issue to grow in size and scope. Hiding from or ignoring the darkness by employing a chemical substance or physical diversion (addiction) can feel like the darkness is abated but the truth becomes illuminated when the masking effect of the addiction is nullified and the person finds their issues are now compounded with the original darkness and, at minimum, healing from the maladies that manifested as a result of their chemical or physical addictions. So what do you do? Obviously you cannot do nothing when fighting darkness but how do overcome something that gets its life force from your reaction?

If you have read this far then here is the answer... you LOVE it.

Hopefully the reader is ready for this simple truth else the reader will find another diversion and move on. For those who are ready then, here is the REAL question... how do you love darkness?

Loving the darkness does NOT mean subjecting yourself to the dark by aligning with it rather it means being grateful for the blessing and wisdom the darkness imparts and giving it your blessing as you send it away. The process of doing so is very similar to the ancient wisdom that states when you find yourself being chased by a monster in your dream, turn around and ask it what it wants. Doing so reclaims the power you gave it so the monster will dissolve before your eyes and allow it to return to its original form so it can deliver the message you refused to hear.

So the BEST way to love the darkness is to ask it what it wants for it is there for your growth and truly does not intend to harm you. Yes the darkness can appear overwhelming and can lead people in to physical and mental maladies including paralysis, psychosis, neurosis, and fatigue but those maladies are the result of your fear and NOT of the messenger.

Another method to "overcome" darkness is to attach the darkness to a decoy and send it to the light. This method will NOT allow you to obtain the wisdom the darkness was called to you to impart (assuming, of course, that the decoy method was NOT the message the messenger was seeking to impart) but it will give you a method to have a temporary reprieve from the darkness that demonstrates the concept of love over battle. The message will return to you, in time, as it is the message you asked to receive, but when "recycled" in this method, you have a side effect way to reclaim the power you granted to the messenger so that the messenger will return in a softer way and present the message in a way similar to the original soft delivery method. A person employing this technique generally is more "advanced" and will recognize when the messenger returns and will accept the message more quicker and more gracefully than in the previous delivery attempt.

Who Cares Analysis	Fear can not and will not abate fear as fear based "motivation" is big business which is very commonly used. Love can not abate fear either despite the common wisdom. Love is NOT the opposite of fear and the invokement of love is NOT a replacement for the lessons and wisdom of fear. Both are two sides of the same coin and the best way to overcome and understand either is to embrace each perspective fully, gracefully, and with gratitude for the blessings and lessons provided by both.

WHAT DOES IT MEAN TO BE "SPIRITUAL"?

I recall a time in which I was the floor supervisor for a 24/7/365.25 (yes a quarter day which is why there is an extra day every four years) call center that was handling the account for a major cell phone carrier. I was happy to be the front line answer guy who handled all the questions for all the departments and would go back on the phones occasionally to make sure I was still up to speed.

One day I got a call from a guy who wanted to fight. I understand he was on hold and may have already been through IVR hell or had some bad information provided so I "took responsibility" and let him vent while I addressed the concern he was calling about. I let him know that I was finished and that everything was correct WELL before he was done ranting so he did all he could to attempt to get me off my game and snidely stated that I just think I know everything. I tolerated his nonsense for a little longer and then tired of it. Since we were required to ask if I had addressed all his questions... you know the inane rhetoric, I presented the question and found he still wanted to fight so I apologized for my inability to address all his concerns adequately and offered to back out everything I had done and put him back in queue so that he may be able to find a representative more on his level who could provide him with the wrong information and experience he needed. At this point I was not concerned with what quality

would state but he decided to take his bad day elsewhere and hung up.

No I do not know everything and I have never made any claims, warrants, or promises that imply or attempt to convey that I know everything. That said, however, I find myself constantly amazed when the all-too-common response I get from someone is they never thought about it like that or they did not know that.

Similarly, I found a post on Facebook that read the paraphrased and sanitized idea that if you do not know the whole story then you should shut up. This was in a group that touts it's spirituality and is extremely typical of those who call themselves spiritual, lightworker, religious, etc. but is a BLATANT example of someone who is a prisoner of the light and is, probably, fighting to stay in quadrant 1.

What such people fail to, or refuse to, understand is that God is EVERYTHING which means that God is good and God is EVIL. Yes... God is both and, at the same time, God is neither. I know those who "live in the light" LOVE to play in the woo-woo stuff, as many Sedona "sensitives" called it, but to understand the WHOLE picture means transversing the Spiritual Time Clock so that you can experience, transcend, and understand the contradictionless contradictions, perfect imperfections, and enlightened darkness instead of just playing in imbalance which is truly being addicted to enslavement.

Those who live in the "woo-woo" will have a VERY hard time with this concept because to them God may be endless parties, a never-ending glass of wine, and unlimited self-adoration for how wonderful of a person they are but, honestly, they are nothing more than spoiled children who refuse to grow up. The "woo-woo" people spend a LOT of time and energy trying to tell everyone that their way – more aptly, the way they were TAUGHT – is the "path of spirituality" and they converse with their circle of friends who act, talk, and dress the same which reinforces the strength of their conviction to their belief as the de facto path that EVERYONE must follow but are BLIND to the understanding that all they are doing is forming another religion. The truth is... EVERY path is a path of spirituality and EVERY path is going to the same destination... at least eventually.

The reader would be wise to question this as this concept does not make sense in the "human" mind. We have been indoctrinated to believe that "authority" is just regardless of action, reciting random nonsense upon demand is "intelligence", and freedom is achieved by following the haphazard and ever-growing "rules" of "society" and that anyone who deviates from this "good citizen" path is bad. It seems completely contra-intuitive that the true hero is sometimes the "bad" person who fights against the system, that those who are deemed as "unintelligible" or mentally inept have wisdom and genius, and the perpetrator who does terrible things can be the catalyst for growth.

So, no you do not need to meditate, be a Breatharian, or do yoga to be spiritual and doing so does NOT make you better or more wise than any one else. The simple truth is that you are ALWAYS spiritual as you are a spiritual being... NOT a biological meat puppet that is the fanciful result of evolution whose thoughts are nothing more than random synapses firing for no reason. What brings you joy is as spiritual as is what brings you terror. You can find your spiritual expression by watching whales breach the water surface just as well as by taking a different route to experience something new.

Who Cares Analysis	Many "spiritual" people have a hard programmed concept that being "spiritual" means being "always in the light" or being, essentially, a listless doormat but neither program is correct. Being "spiritual" implies, in my opinion, being authentic. Yes there are times when "holding light" for a person, group, event, etc. is being "spiritual" just as punching a dictator in the mouth can be "spiritual". Allowing people to abuse you or treat you badly is NOT spiritual, loving, or compassionate and should NOT be tolerated. Loving boundaries and honest emotions can help you attune in to yourself at a deeper level than following the herd and doing whatever the "woo-woo" instructor says. The path to follow is YOUR path... your individual path that can, at times, include the herd but, more often than not, will lead you towards your own unique version of spirituality which is TRULY being spiritual.

HOW TO SPOT A FAKE

Everything hurt and I felt like I was on fire. My body felt like it was being ripped apart and I thought I crapped my bed when I was awoken from a deep sleep only to find myself in the midst of this terrifying experience. I barely had time to look at the alarm clock before it was over and I passed out. It was not until later that morning when my alarm clock woke me to begin the day that I learned that my cousin had been in a fatal accident during the night.

The day before was my daughter's birthday and spirit had warned me that she was not going to live beyond that birthday a few months prior so I made sure I spent all the time I could with her until her birthday and I did not allow her out of my sight on her birthday. Yes, I watched her from the midnight of her birthday until the next midnight the day after her birthday to ensure I would be there in case something happened… nothing did and I felt I had dodged a bullet when I went to bed victorious only to be awoken as described above.

I did my best to get ready for work but my daughter's mother asked me why I was staring at the TV since it was off. I had no idea that the TV was off as I was clearly seeing an accident scene on the screen but I did not understand why I was seeing this until I got the call from my aunt who wanted to let me know that my cousin had been killed in a car crash and some of the details of what happened… her description matched what

I was seeing and then I understood that I was watching my cousin's death and the trauma of my cousin's death matched what I felt, meaning I took the pain from my cousin.

I was confounded with emotions that I did not know how to balance. On one hand I was ecstatic that I "beat" the spirit warning concerning my daughter but, on the other, my cousin – my <u>favorite</u> cousin – was killed. This is the cousin who helped my through my own darkness. Darkness that was so strong that no one could be around me. I recall a time in which I projected such darkness that I became completely removed from human interaction. I was so dark that even "bad" guys wouldn't engage me. I recall an incident when I purposely walked through a group of guys in order to entice any type of contact, hostile preferred, and the one guy who too busy trying to entertain his friends, felt my aura and yelled "Oh Jesus" when he quickly – and literally – jumped out of my aura. So although I was left to fester in my own darkness… this is the cousin – and the ONLY person – who loved me anyways.

I was very happy and thankful to have my cousin's spirit come to thank me for taking the pain of the death and I was able to accompany my cousin to the "doorway" between the realms before my cousin crossed over. I call it a doorway for lack of better euphemism but, for me at least, it is not a doorway. What I see when

I have accompanied other loved ones to the "great divide" is best understood as a brilliant light in space which is where the souls return home to once they willingly enter. Despite all of this time with my cousin, I was ill prepared for the wisdom that my cousin had died in place of my daughter which entered in to my mind shortly before my cousin's funeral.

I am not sure how or when my cousin made the decision to go home in place of my daughter or why she did. I am not sure if this was a "nexus" point (a preplanned potential exit point) in their life plans or if someone asked my cousin to take my daughter's place but this realization really bedazzled my thin iced emotions and then came the gypsy.

The family was at my cousin's funeral when my aunt said she needed to talk to me. Apparently a gypsy had arrived – uninvited – and had told my aunt that she (the gypsy) could bring my cousin back to life for whatever money value. Now before the reader begins whining about me calling this person a gypsy and finding it offensive... deal with it! The area where this occurred was KNOWN to have psychics who called themselves gypsies so it was NOT unheard of to have someone arrive claiming to be a gypsy. I immediately wanted to meet this person as I wanted to test the gypsy's power by having her bring herself back to life after I killed her. Yes the audacity of someone to come to the funeral of a young person and make false claims was TOO much for me and I was ready for a demonstration. My aunt told me that people had already kicked the gypsy out but came to talk to me personally as my reaction was predicted and the family wanted to protect me from making a bad emotional decision.

There are a TON of fake readers out there who are solely interested in telling you whatever you want to hear in order to make money. Many of the gypsy variety, for example, will begin by telling you that you are cursed, your family is cursed, or there is a dark energy around you that only they can get rid of but their fee, for such advanced work or spiritually "dangerous" work, would be several hundred or thousands of dollars. Other "professional" readers are under the gun to sell as many readings as possible and will give you cookie cutter gibberish that is often led by your answers and feature very easy to spot sweeping generalizations, stereotyped biases, and psychobabble.

Who Cares Analysis	Getting an intuitive reading is a highly personal experience which typically costs a considerable amount of money that, of course and unfortunately, attracts scammers whose only interest is your money. Such scammers essentially cut their own throats as their short sighted profiteering comes at the cost of longevity by losing the customer and sowing the seeds of distrust for future readings. True intuitive services are provided by professionals who ask very little yet grant a bevy of poignant and verifiable information that one cannot know or state at random. Such information can help guide the client along its path and illuminate the meaning of situations when things are confused or blurred. A truthful intuitive will encourage the client to review the information provided against their own intuition opposed to making the client dependent.

HOW HISTORY IS WRITTEN

I recall seeing a thing on Facebook in which the great-grandchildren of Georg Johannes Ludwig Ritter von Trapp sang Edelweiss. For those who don't know, the story of von Trapp's escape from Nazi controlled Austria is presented in the movie the "Sound of Music" in which the character who portrays von Trapp sings Edelweiss so the real life great-grandchildren's rendition of the song is homage to the family's culture. How accurate the movie is does not matter at this time as the movie itself is a version of history so do not ask me about the historical accuracy as I neither know or care. While my bias on the escapade of von Trapp is exposed by me inscribing escape, there are those out there who find his defection to be inexcusable and, thus, is the basis of history.

History, in general, is highly biased propaganda that is written by the victors so von Trapp is extremely lucky that the Nazi's lost else the story portrayed in the "Sound of Music" would be MUCH different. In fact, it is not difficult to imagine the Nazi version of von Trapp's travels as being somewhat akin to the treatment of ANY person who dares to question the dictatorial government as the movie would be composed as and celebrated as a warning to anyone else who dared to even think about defection.

In many cases, history is written and controlled by governmental military forces as they seek to promote their cause and whitewash their misdeeds in a highly embellished, sanitized, and grossly Pollyanna stylized caricature that maximizes their image and utility in their culture. Such romanced versions of history are well debated by songs like the late Floyd Red Crow Westerman's "Custer Died for Your Sins" and Blackfire's "Exile". I know most of the readers have never heard either of these songs – or the artists – but they paint the trials and tribulations of Native Americans in a much darker – and probably more accurate – picture then what is recorded in history books as, once again, the invaders who conquered (with better weapons) the land of the ancestors are the ones who books got published in their culture… the culture of the conquerors. Yes there are some protests and tomes that are inscribed by the conquered but their wisdom is rarely heard by the "social justice warriors" who are so apt to fight for any oppression that is convenient for them.

It is this propagandized sanitation and white washing that allows many of the young adults in a given society to envision the concept of "serving one's country" as something other than thuggery as it romanticizes the concept of killing the enemy as a glorious endeavor and entices (many) recruits with promises of better money and benefits via a thinly veiled job-training program that is little more than a way to attract bodies which, typically, come from a less financially blessed socioeconomic sample of the population. The sad reality is that both sides of the battlefield are typically fighting for the EXACT same reason and with the exact same – or VERY similar – propaganda.

I am sure the above paragraph – if allowed by the censors – will get some panties in a bunch by a bunch of indoctrinated people who would likely find von Trapp an insufferable traitor and who claim to fight for freedom while actively demanding unwavering compliance with their thoughts and carte blanche for their actions by citing the unpardonable excuse of ANY version of "just following orders" but for those who are able to consider another point of view... I will outline the horrors of war.

No, in this experience I did not have to be on the front lines of a battlefield as I have already spent enough time killing and being killed in previous experiences and several memories of such endeavors remain. I have, however, been bullied by all kinds of "enemy combatants" throughout my childhood but rather than dwell on the lessons these dark teacher conveyed, I thank them for their teaching and have moved on; unfortunately, not all are so lucky.

To the dismay of those who seek to threaten me and my current experience for the free speech and accurate comments made above, they should know that I was a primary in the opening of a veteran's charity which was conceived to help wounded veterans. I did this NOT because I support the inane BS that veterans are spoon fed in order to willingly put themselves in harm's way but because I have seen the extreme mental, physical, and spiritual maladies these people suffer... often for the rest of their current experience and I wanted to help alleviate their suffering. My step-grandfather was one of them.

My step-grandfather was an interesting character. He was, essentially, a drifter who never met a get-rich scheme that he did not like or try. He was the guy who would purchase a lot of whatever miracle product that was advertised on television and take it to market to sell. He made a meager living from sales endeavors but it kept him in beer, cigarettes, and coffee so he was happy... until he would go to sleep. He had been in war (which war does NOT matter) and had killed the enemy as it was his job and "duty" to do. He was honorably discharged and had certain medals but he was never able to forgive himself for what he did and would often wake himself by screaming he was sorry and urinating on himself when the ghosts of the enemy came to visit him as he slept. It did not seem that the ghosts were there to harm him as he mentioned that they would routinely reach out to him and say they forgave him but he would relive the killing scenes and did not like what he saw. This, of course, is why he was mentally incapable of holding a "steady" job and why he would consume upwards of 20 beers a day.

As a natural healer, I would do my best to help him accept, understand, and forgive but he was never ready. I was able to see and speak with the spirits of those he killed and confirmed they were trying to help him forgive himself but, again, he was not ready and, sadly, remained not ready for the rest of his experience. Thankfully, he did find some level of understanding when he was able to reflect on his experience from the "other side" but, most likely, will have another experience in which he revisits a similar circumstance in order to achieve the wisdom he was unable to achieve throughout his long term self medication.

I am sure that if my step-grandfather were to have written a book, his version of his main growth challenge would be, remarkably, similar to the growth challenge of one of the soldiers he killed but the words of the peasants are of little concern or value to those who send each soldier to war... unless the words can be used to promote whatever some politician is trying to sell.

I recall being at a friend's house in Georgia where I came across a book in my friend's bookcase that had the title of "The Real Reason for the Civil War" - or something to that effect. As a student of "forbidden" knowledge and history, I was immediately intrigued and decided to read the book. It was wonderful to read a book that was outside of the cultural norm and it did paint the "rationale" for the Civil War in a light that is NOT taught in any school that I have attended. The accuracy of the book would be difficult to verify as it is a book that was written by the losing army and it promoted it's viewpoint with the same bias and apple-polishing of its "heroes" as the victor's but there certainly is the same level of truth as there is in any biased document.

Who Cares Analysis	Historical accuracy is a point of contention and it is prudent to help the reader understand why it is good to consider the alternative point of view. It is commonly held that there are two sides to every story but that is often not the case as each side understands its truth from its unique perspective meaning that there are, at least, three sides to every conflict – truth from perspective A, truth from perspective B, and the truth. Such understanding that both side are, typically, fighting for the same promises and reasons should make the reader pause and reflect on their programming and triggers so that both can be exposed and expunged.

UNCONDITIONAL LOVE

This is one of the most unreasonable expectations of the human mythology but one that is commonly cited by those in quadrant 1 so we will explore the lunacy of unconditional love herein.

There really is no model for the understanding of unconditional love in the human paradigm. There are several mythos which explore the concept but none seem to be able to obtain this unobtainable and lofty ideal. Some people claim that their pets love them unconditionally but this is not true as the master/slave, owner/pet, parent/child relationship – choose the one you prefer – that is inherent with pets (assuming the person takes care of the pets… many do not) IS a conditional relationship that is based on dependency. Others claim that their children love them unconditionally but there is seemingly incalculable amount of evidence to the contrary which shows parents and children doing terrible things to the other regardless of how either was treated or raised.

Religion does not have ANY model either as many churches will tell you that "God" is not unconditional love rather "God" is "just" implying that whatever "God" does is OK because "God" is beyond the law of "God". Further, "God" itself displays this lack of unconditional love not just in the times that "God" killed all the firstborn children, sent a flood to destroy ALL of humanity, or created Hell to punish ALL who dare to eat shellfish,

get a tattoo, or who disobey "authority" but in the times when "God" said that "God" was a "jealous God" while citing jealousy (yes I understand that the actual terminology is envy but jealousy is often cited as a synonym for envy and is used interchangeably) as one of the deadly sins. Obviously this means that the "God" of the Bible is not able to model unconditional love.

The internet does little to assist in this quandary as depending on the website, there are either 4, 7, or 8 types of love and not one of them are unconditional. Yes… I understand that there are some that seem like unconditional but let's explore a scenario to test the unconditional theory. Be warned… this may be a bit spicy…

The mythos of unconditional love says your love for another will continue steadfast and remain static despite what another – typically someone special to you in your life – does or says to you. Using this logic… imagine coming home after a long day of soul sucking work only to find your other actively and passionately engaged in "adult activities" with your best friend, your most beloved relative, and all other takers in your neighborhood simultaneously and your other doesn't even acknowledge you when you make a reasonable demand for the act to stop. Or… you are resting peacefully with your other in bed and you see your other get out of bed and get something from behind the dresser in your room. You think your other is getting something romantic so you relax and try to recoil in horror as you find your body engulfed in liquid fire and unimaginable pain as your beloved other has doused you with acid.

I am sure there are those who are running now to write emails, blogs, and letters to whomever to demand answers on how a spiritual book could dare include such horrific concepts but while you may be mad, shocked, appalled, or offended (you're welcome) ... a reasonable person would admit that my brief (and purposely overblown) scenarios were effective in triggering some emotions and to make you see how most would – reasonably – react in such a circumstance and how unrealistic the concept of unconditional love is. With that... I cannot imagine ANY person not having some issue with a circumstance of a similar nature but that is what the mythos of unconditional love suggests... that someone would encounter and endure such an event (hopefully MUCH less in substance although it is possible to experience worse) and NOT have a change in how they see or feel about the other and I am reasonably sure that the reader would agree with me. Now here is the kicker... unconditional love DOES exist!

Real unconditional love, despite all of the evidence and rationale to the contrary DOES exist and such love is freely and forever available to ALL without condition, limitation, or barrier. This is a major conundrum to most as unconditional love is not understood in "society". In fact, and sadly, the closest most get to the concept of unconditional love is the oxymoronic mythology that the "Godhead" will forgive all your sins, transgressions, shortcomings, mistakes, etc. (that it created and already knows before you do) and love you "unconditionally" and for eternity provided one condition... that you wash yourself in the blood of its fractal "son" and accept this portion of the "Godhead" as your lord and master. Such lunacy is understood when the reader understands that such infallibility is found everywhere is science as there is always an exception to a scientific law regardless of discipline.

Despite the lack of understanding of the true meaning of unconditional love, the good news for those who are "lost" (quadrant 2) or looking for "redemption" (quadrant 3) is that there is NOTHING you can do, say, or manifest to make the real God love you any less and conversely the bad news for the "lightworkers" (quadrant 1) who are so engulfed in their "divine" actions is that there is NOTHING you can do, say, or manifest to make the real God love you any more. The real God – the God YOU are a part of – IS unconditional love.

Who Cares Analysis	Ultimately, and if we are being honest, most of what people are doing with their lives is either doing "good works" to to make the invisible "father in the sky" happier with them in order to gain favor and "blessings" or to hide from the "judge in the sky" due to some real, imagined, or feared error that happened at some point in their existence so that they are not cast to Hell. Those who engage in selling this paradigm are also trying to sell you its "cure" for 10% of your income without question or end and have done terrible things throughout history to all in its way and under its control. There is no need for ANY of this but it is your choice. You are fully in control over what you allow to control you and have power over you. You now have truthful information that is biased in its intent to free you from your accepted confides. Choose wisely.

HEAVEN AND HELL ARE PERSPECTIVES

Heaven, in general, is a societal concept that expounds the best of the culture to its inhabitants whose promise is often used as a governor to instill obedience, the right to rule, and other state preferences. Christians, from a Western consumer based culture, are programmed to expect Heaven to be a place filled with streets of gold which is surrounded by pearly gates where one worships "God" forever and is accessible, contingently, to those who accept a fractal of "God" as "God". American Natives, on the other hand, tend to view Heaven as a large field that is full of game and natural wonders... of course this depends on the tribe but, generally, a Native perspective will be more natural. The Norse of Norse mythology, however and during their days of exploration and conquest, viewed Heaven (Valhalla) as an enormous banquet hall where the warriors who died in the most "glorious" battle go to be rewarded for the "valor" and to prepare to fight against the enemies of Asgard during Ragnarok. The promise of the "good life" after a life of servitude is a good way to get a peasant to submit to the will of the state and sacrifice themselves in war.

Hell, on the other hand, tends to be a place that is filled with those a person does not like and where the temperature is either "Hot as Hell" or "Cold as Hell" depending on the person and society. Dante Alighieri's infamous poem, the Divine Comedy, for example, is well known to be filled with people Dante did not like throughout his nine circles of Hell.

Interestingly, a book in the fictional Star Wars series, Apocalypse, views Heaven and Hell as the same place where the person's energy finds a level which best resonates with their "level" where their energy will reside. Such description matches well with many New Age philosophies and is echoed on this plane as the perspective of Heaven and Hell depends on the viewpoint of the observer as each exist simultaneously.

My Heaven, for example, would be meeting my best friend on the racquetball court using bo staffs in place of racquetball racquets and ready for the full contact experience whereas my best friend's Hell would finding me ready to "play" on a racquetball court! Such is the difference in personal perspective... what is joyful, fun, and a life changing experience to one person is an annoying, pointless, and inane task to another. Both perspectives are right and both are wrong but both perspectives exist simultaneously and it is the opinion of the observer that assigns the valuation difference based, solely, on their perspective.

Who Cares Analysis	To some the smell of a rose is a sweet fragrant smell that ranks high on their chart of pleasures where as to allergy sufferers the smell of a rose can be a histamine nightmare filled with headaches, nasal congestion, and drainage. The acceptance or rejection of anything and everything is solely and completely up to the perspective of the observer echoing the wisdom that "It does not matter what happens to you. What matters is how you deal with it." Whatever challenge you find yourself in, no matter how difficult you allow it to be to overcome, it remains as strong or as weak as you deem it. Your perspective truly affects everything and you always have the ability to choose what you see.

FREQUENTLY ASKED QUESTIONS

What came first the chicken or the egg?

This simple question is presented here to illustrate to the reader how I think differently then most as this has simple mind twister has puzzled people for some time but I answered it in elementary school. The answer I gave then, as now, is the egg because dinosaurs laid eggs LONG before chickens existed. Now if the question was the chicken or the chicken egg then that would be a very different question and in that scenario... I would still have to choose the chicken as, biologically, the chicken was identified and named before its method of reproduction was discovered so the answer would have to remain, chicken.

Why do bad things happen to good people?

The answer to this often asked question is as simple as it is infuriating... for your growth. Everything that happens to you is done so with your express allowance (typically before the current incarnation although you can make vows, pacts, and contracts while incarnated that are carried over throughout multiple incarnations) in order to allow you to experience what it is that you seek to experience. Many of the challenges the reader is currently listing in their head – as they curse me for such a ridiculous postulate – does NOT make sense when viewed through human eyes but this is true nonetheless.

Does energy medicine always work?

Energy medicine does work if the recipient allows it to with acceptance being either an express acknowledgment of allowance or if the acceptance is in their life plan.

I was flying either to or from DC one year – which way is irrelevant – when a little girl was brought in to the waiting area on a stretcher. She was flanked by her parents and then by a group of people asking about the child and her condition offering their condolences and prayers. What the ailment of the child was I do not know as I never asked and, honestly, did not care as I well know that what the well intended group was doing was actually FANNING the fire of the child's ailment so I kept my distance. I could see the child was in pain and listless so I – without the consent of the child – began a distance healing and it failed. I received the message that I could not remove the ailment from the child as this is the growth opportunity she incarnated to overcome. I understood that I was unable to proceed as doing so would be a direct violation of the child's sovereignty but I was able to ease her pain temporarily as this was allowed by her plan so I switched my intention from disease abatement to pain relief and the effect was instantaneous and very plain to see. The eye's of the little girl began to brighten and she began to smile. She turned to me and I felt she was just about to express her thanks so I sent her the message that I did not want to be seen so please don't but I am glad you are feeling better. With that, she smiled and sat up much to the surprise and joy of her family.

The little girl was very happy to receive the pain relief but there are others who dwell in their pain and find their "identity" therein and have no intention or desire to be freed from their chains despite their, typically, loud statements to the contrary. The best illustration that most people understand is the disease creation programming statement that "I can't help you until you admit that you have a problem". Yes, I understand that there are TONS of people out there who well fit the adage that "misery loves company" and who are unable to see themselves as an addict but the pendulum is far too imbalanced to the point that, in my opinion, MANY "modern" diseases are nothing more than marketing tools to drive drug sales. No I am not going to bash mental health system as they are doing the best they can to give some level of relief to the souls suffering in a toxic culture but most mental health practitioners are so far in the forest that they cannot see the trees or, in this case, MANY times they are unable to see that they are enablers opposed to healers.

I have counseled mental health practitioners who are so focused on meeting government and agency key performance indicators and incentive programs that they BECOME the patient as they are unable to live the advice they give and it takes a terrible toll on their mental and physical state.

While I have witnessed energy medicine being deployed as "Traditional Healing" in some native health systems and have heard that the energy healing modality known as "Reiki" is being allowed and somewhat accepted in private health systems, overall and generally speaking, energy medicine remains confined in the realm of "snake oil" as people are programmed to reject it as such. It is laughable that energy medicine is called "new age" when many modalities are FAR older than "modern" medicine which actually makes "modern" medicine the new age and energy medicine the establishment but I am sure the reader is already having issue with this statement which serves to underscore the programming. Still, due to this programming, many reject energy medicine until they have exhausted or tire of the never ending drug/side effect cycle of "modern" medicine and seek true relief opposed to being a cog in the "disease management" profit cycle. Even then the success of energy medicine is wholly dependent on the person's allowance of the treatment and many scoff at the simple treatment and reject it… which is their innate and sovereign right.

I asked for help… why didn't it come?

The answer to this is simple but the understanding is somewhat convoluted… at least in human eyes. The easy, simple, and truest answer is… help did come. Now for the convoluted part… it may not have come in the form you want, expected, or recognize.

There are way too many scenarios to limit this explanation to a simple, generalized answer so the answer has to include some questions. Such questions include whom did you ask, what did you ask them to do, did you allow them to assist, and is it the right time?

It sounds ludicrous to consider who you asked but people, especially when they are frustrated, can just ask thin air for help and not to anyone or anything in particular in order to release frustration. To elicit help, you need to address the request to someone or something directly so that the being or group can receive the question and listen. Some people will say that this needs to be done verbally due to the intention behind the verbalization but I have always found this step to be unnecessary as such dictate would negate the intention and authority of the mute. I will not go too deep in to why at this point but in summation… ALL is energy and limiting a request to a VERY small portion of the electromagnetic spectrum is nonsensical so, in my opinion and in my experience, your non-verbal request is heard just as loud – if not louder – and is understood just as well as a verbal request.

This does not mean, however, that you need to know exactly whom to address the request to. Making a basic request to your "Guardian Angel", for example, is a good enough catalyst to begin the process as the Guardian Angel knows you intimately and well understands your mannerisms, needs, and communication style to correctly receive, interpret, and process your request to the correct channels on the other side. Yes, while we like to think that whatever language we speak in our head is understood universally, such is NOT the case as whatever language we communicate with is very limited and is highly dependent on how we speak and our enunciation among a wide gaggle of other factors few, of which, are spoken in spirit.

With the proper receipt and delivery of your request the request is granted and the answer is returned but the answer may not be in a manner you expect or allow. I know I have questioned this myself and have, in anger, demanded to know why the universe – with all of its resources, wisdom, and timelessness – cannot simply send me an answer via email.

Honestly, with my IT security background, and to answer my own question, even if the universe DID email me, I would, most likely, mark the email as SPAM and never even open it. So the universe will communicate the answer to you through other means.

There was a time, for example, in which my daughter was in a very dark place and I was extremely frustrated with just about everything. Some hard choices were on the horizon and my mindset was dark. It was in a time of despair that I received a surprise call from a school my daughter used to attend. The receptionist told me that she got a message for me from my grandmother who said that everything would be fine and it is ok to relax. The school receptionist was very confused about the message and really did not know where it came from. I, on the other hand, was very grateful for the message as my grandmother was dead and knew that part of the issue was my daughter's current school so it was with great wisdom that the call came from a school where things had been good as it was highly unlikely that I would take a call from the current school.

Many people really have trouble allowing the answer to come as we like to live in the illusion that we know MUCH more than we do and that we are in control so it is often the case that the requested solution is trying to come through but we are too stubborn or ignorant to allow it to manifest. In my case, for example, I had been told that moving to Arizona would be the turning point in my life. I resisted this message for years continually questioning the message and the concept of moving to Arizona. I thought I was well educated and knew FAR more than I did so all I can say is that when I finally did listen and made the move to Arizona, I found my life did indeed change and I wish I had listened sooner. Of course I had to go when

I and the situation were ready which introduces one of my least favorite concepts... right timing.

Right timing, better known as Divine Timing, is a concept that I have battled for many years and it is highly likely that the reader can relate but, once again, this boils down to ignorance and control. Just because we think, in human eyes, we know what we want – and we want it now – does NOT mean that the immediate delivery of the request would be in our best interest as such delivery may violate our spiritual growth which would immediately prevent the delivery of the request. Anything externally that prevents you from your growth challenge – no matter what the intention – is NOT helping you and is depriving you of the ability to find your own unique path in your own unique way as is your divine expression choice. You have the ability, within yourself, to be successful in whatever growth challenge you accepted else you would not be able to accept the challenge(s) – without exception – and everything you need to successfully overcome a stepping stone will arrive when you are ready to utilize the tool and NOT before. No amount of whining, bargaining, demanding, or pouting will change this or make this happen ANY faster than you allow it by being ready. I know... I've tried.

How can I obtain the title of Christ?

Assuming the mythological Christian entity known as Jesus is NOT simply a plagiarized mishmash of other ancient mythological beings that were commonly known in its region of origin – which there is CONSIDERABLE evidence for, it would be nice to call Jesus by his REAL name.

First and foremost... it is NOT Jesus Christ.

The title of Christ is a title that is achieved through enlightenment and the transcendence of "reality" which is, in effect and purpose, nearly identical to the title of and meaning of Buddha. While the pious sheeple would turn a disdainful eye towards the name Jesus the Buddha, such nomenclature is FAR more accurate and respectful than the erroneous colloquial vernacular of Jesus Christ.

Now before I am inundated with people telling me I am also wrong... yes, I know. The actual title is Christos NOT Christ. Personally I do NOT care about the name attributed to this unbelievable being that is alleged to have performed all of these miracles in front of extremely large groups of people but is NOT recorded by ANY of the scholars of the era in ANY document. In our era, even people with no discernible talent can be thoroughly documented and photographed by ALL sorts of people for ALL sorts of reason and while such technology did NOT exist in those days, people are people and it seems HIGHLY unlikely and improbable that a miraculous being, such as Jesus the Christ, does NOT appear in ANY document from ANY person until HUNDREDS of years after it's alleged death.

It is more reasonable that the crafting of such a super being was conceived for the same reason super heroes were created in the '40s... to rally public opinion in to an easy to control focal point via a fictional character that endowed with superhuman powers and abilities which the fictional super being employs to overcome ALL obstacles no matter how insurmountable. In those days, fictional characters like the indestructible Superman and the thinly veiled military superman, Captain America, were developed to bring hope and the "indomitable American fighting spirit" to the troops that were hopelessly fighting or enlisting in to the soon to start WWII. Statistics indicate that, historically, super hero movies increase in popularity as societal depression increases an indication that well supports my point and is something currently observed as America falls to totalitarianism, in part, amongst its staggering and insurmountable national debt and lack of trust in elected "officials". It goes without saying that the lives of these fictional super heroes are FAR better recorded and documented than the alleged life of the original fictional Super Man; Jesus the Christ.

Those tangents aside… how does one obtain the title of Christ?

First and foremost one needs to understand what the title of Christ means. Depending on the translation used, the term christ means "messiah" or the "anointed one". The dissemination of the title of christ allegedly infers a special relationship with "God". In the case of the caricature illustrated in the, supposed, historically accurate and infallible dogma of Western Religion, the being colloquially – and improperly – called Jesus Christ is alleged to be the only son of "God" while simultaneously being a third of "God". While the concept of the eternal "creator" of everything being limited to a sole child (reproduction implies a life cycle while negates the concept of eternal life) is laughable and the concept of living multiple lives simultaneously disavows the dogmatic concept of one life to live thereby granting credence to metaphysical and quantum entanglement (sorry nerds!), the truth is, as the Jesus character is documented, that we are ALL children of "God" and we ALL can do all that he can… and more.

I was born bad… there is no hope for me

There is, ultimately, no good or bad as both are perspectives and while this wisdom sounds sagely and is easy to type, the reality is that there are some of the first programs we ingest and are, therefore, VERY palatable in the "real world" experience. In foster care I personally witnessed wonderful, gifted people allow themselves to believe they were broken, worthless scumbags whose future was highly likely to include homelessness, addiction, and long term incarceration. I did not witness the same programming in non-foster kids. Yes they still had their challenges but there is a HUGE difference between threatening to run away or kill yourself because you did not get the tablet or car you wanted compared to the person who is completely frustrated because all they hear are "these are the best years of your life" and life has truly sucked to that point and they see little change in the future.

Many of the people I have explained the basis of the Spiritual Time Clock have been foster kids which means that many have been on the streets or in jail or prison and are desperately seeking help. It is wonderful to see the rekindling of light in their sullen and darkened eyes but, typically, the negative programming is what they are accustomed to and, therefore, is what they relate to and believe. Regardless, the fact remains that those who are born with the greatest darkness are typically the most "advanced" and in a soon to "graduate" class. Being "awarded" with these "blessings" implies they are able to accomplish their challenges and no matter what growth challenge success or failures they incur… they have the ability to succeed provided they shake the programming and find their light and truth inside.

The key to unlocking this light is responsibility. Yes, this is a concept that most run far away from but when a person accepts their true nature and takes personal responsibility for everything, they find they are no longer enslaved to and in "societal" norms (programming) which frees them from all self imposed and societal sanctioned concepts, expectations, and limitations. No, the process of deprogramming does not, typically, happen overnight as people find they need to overcome layers of programming which are, often, intertwined with emotions and memories that are "exercised" one day at a time.

The belief that you were born "good" or "bad" are societal limitations that a person "wears" in order to play and ascribe to their "role" but whatever label you choose to allow society or yourself to place onto you is your responsibility of which you are in complete control. Choice is the ultimate form of responsibility and your right to choose (aka free will) is ALWAYS available to you should you choose to accept it and the responsibilities that come with knowing you are the controller of your destiny… whatever destiny you choose to pursue. Many prefer to accept the asinine concept that someone else is in control of their lives as this takes their real, perceived, and imagined failures out of their responsibility but such "luxury" has the cost of your freedom.

Those who are blessed with an overwhelming load – especially at an early age – are ready to move to the next level of love provided they look inside and take responsibility for their growth challenges no matter what label society places on these concepts.

What did I do to deserve this?

This is one that does not make sense in human terms. As incarnate beings, we are programmed to revere wealth and to idolize whomever appears that way even if they are simply "faking it until they make it". The fun part is that what we hold such reverence for in human eyes typically holds little value or interest in spiritual eyes and this is one of those conundrums. While we are trained to hold those who have hoarded and value wealth (whatever form the wealth takes in the society) as the infallible and unerring pillars of society, truth be told, many who hoard wealth do so out of low level fear and, generally, - NOTE I stated generally – are not far along the Spiritual Time Clock.

No this does NOT mean that everyone who has money is bad nor does it imply – in ANY manner – that those who do not have money are good or vice versa. I have, personally, known wonderful, loving, and gregarious people with and without money as I have known selfish, conniving, and spiteful people with and without money. Money is NOT the root of all evil and money is simply a tool so stop basing your viewpoint on people based on their perceived financial "status" and accept them for who they are.

Whatever circumstance you find yourself in is a direct reflection of your growth and the challenges you accepted before incarnation. Some of us, myself included, came with past experience programs in which we had negative viewpoints of wealth which prevented the accumulation of wealth and rendered us homeless wondering why and what I did to deserve this. Sound familiar?

As I write this I find the financial leaning somewhat interesting and wonder how many readers will share this viewpoint but this question is NOT mutually exclusive to the domain of finances as the person pondering this can be in any number of personal "Hells" and are needing to find balance in order to move forward. To this, and in consideration of the immeasurable number of applicable situations and variables, the best I can can provide is to reiterate the wisdom (albeit annoying wisdom when presented) that you are not given more than you can handle so the good news is that you have the capacity to overcome whatever you are facing and the bad news is… it is up to you to do so.

Why am I here?

All of us are beings of light that have come "here" to learn and experience whatever lessons and experiences we want. Some are here to simply party, some are here to grow, and some are here to help others grow. We know our "mission" before we incarnate and this remembrance helps guide us throughout our current experience no matter how much or how little we can recall this "consciously". We have been programmed to believe in the concept of destiny and a lot of hoopla surrounds the mystique of destiny but what you are destined to do pales in comparison with your true mission… to experience.

What books or songs helped me in my experience?

This is a quick summary of books or songs that were relevant to me at a very challenging point and what I have referenced to push through a block. This is not meant to be an exhaustive inventory as such a list would certainly span volumes and read like the mind numbing and coma inducing genealogy of another person.

- Ancient Wisdom: The Dead Sea Scrolls
- Book: The Way of the Peaceful Warrior, Dan Millman
- Book: What to do when you are Dead, Craig Hamilton-Parker
- Song: Walk on Faith, Mike Reid

- Song: Coming Out of the Dark, Gloria Estefan
- Song: As Long as I can Dream, Expose
- Song: Just as I am, Various including Hymnal, Air Supply, and Ricky van Shelton
- Song: Come on In, Oak Ridge Boys
- Song: That's what Love is For, Amy Grant
- Song: Let your Love Flow, Bellamy Brothers
- Song: Just Remember I Love You, Firefall
- Song: Love Without End, Amen, George Strait

What is Empath Backup?

Empath Backup occurs when an empath ingests too much volatile energy and begins feeling frustrated, angry, and dark and finds themselves ready to give back with interest. Empath Backup can be balanced by the empath spending time alone in nature, around large bodies of water, meditation, or any other solo activity that removes the empath from the energy source(s) but, unfortunately, such is not understood in "healthcare" or supported in "modern" day society whose healing mantra tends to be, "Here is a drug. Get back to work".

Emapath Backup is a REAL malady that plagues empathic people but is not addressed as a real disease in favor of a gaggle of lessor psychobabble components and flavor of the month ailments. The unfortunate empaths that seek advice of the system to help balance themselves often wind up FAR worse then they were previously as the tools deployed to mask the symptoms do nothing to solve the issue and being held in a facility full of distress only exacerbates the empath backup further and creates a vicious cycle that mandates additional "support". While it is true that such a Hellish nightmare may be exactly the darkness the empath <u>needs</u> to learn balance and break out of this vicious cycle, those who are not ready can find themselves locked up in a shell – of their own design – that is difficult for them to release themselves from.

It is imperative for the empath to learn boundaries in order to function normally and to be able to serve in the capacity they seek as being able to step away and balance is not always an option in "life". Boundaries will allow the empath to have a real time threshold to gauge when they are entering in to the empath backup (red line) zone so they can do whatever necessary to reduce the pressure and regain control.

Growing up Empath

Growing up as an empath can be a daunting task. The empath child can feel and be influenced by the emotions surrounding the child which can make the child appear to be wishy-washy, attention deficit, withdrawn, or a gaggle of similar psychobabble none of which are well understood or supported in society. The female empath child is much better tolerated and accepted in society than the male empath child but the empath child, regardless of gender or gender identification, will need to master balance to control when and where they absorb the energy of those around them but most, especially if they are not supported, do all they can to repress their "odd" behavior in order to function "normally" in society. As expected, such suppression is highly toxic and can manifest serious challenges as the emapthic nature seeks to return to the surface.

A native foster brother of mine was supported and accepted by his tribe and lived happily therein serving as a caller and a healer. He was told of a neighboring tribe who was starving so he went to the village to investigate and found the tribe was unable to catch any fish and the sustenance hunting time was coming to a close soon. He went to the ocean to "call" for help and the starving village was eating very well the same night. I know most of the readers will want to question this as this is something foreign to most non-native cultures so rather than give you all the answers... I will invite you to do your own research in to the culture should this really put a bunch in your panties.

Unfortunately, the problems started when he tried to balance his abilities with the religious control structure of the macro-culture and was programmed to believe his skills were "evil".

He took the programming to heart and began to hate and fear every part of himself leading to decades of homelessness, self-medicating, and virtual enslavement by unscrupulous interests who knew of his skills and controlled him by feeding his addictions. At one point he was actually traveling the wilderness and scrying for gold using nothing but his connection to the land and was making his "employer" a fortune while being provided as much self-medication as he wanted as remittance for his service. It was his desire to be accepted by the macro-culture that was the catalyst for his movement on the spiritual time clock and in to darkness and he has suffered greatly as he remains stuck and is unwilling to move towards his dark night.

It is both tragic and a blessing that MANY – if not MOST – empaths are NOT well received in the macro-culture but this is because the macro-culture is inherently toxic and this is one of the very challenges the empath came to experience and transcend. Having worked in a psychiatric hospital, I have personally witnessed the treatment of empaths in the macro-culture whose answer to everything is to take a drug and get back to productivity.

I recall a person whose light was extremely bright but the person was suffering from a TON of others who were attached and draining the person dry. The solution of the macro-culture was to severely sedate the person to treat the "psychosis" and to isolate the person with psychobabble and "treatment" but the person was not getting better. I had to wait until I felt the energy of the person ask me for help and then I took the person aside and explained to the person that I understood the person's heart and intent were of the highest purpose but givers give and takers take and takers will take EVERYTHING and MORE unless you have clear boundaries. I knew the person wanted to help others and felt bad about removing the parasites as the person was concerned what would happen to them so I told the person that until this is in place the "change" the macro-culture wants to see will NOT occur and to consider how many people you are not able to help because you are allowing these parasites to drain you completely. The person did as I outlined and was soon discharged leaving the macro-culture to ponder how the person went from severely mentally ill to a productive member of society seemingly overnight. I am sure the macro-culture chalked up the success to some drug of the moment in conjunction with their infallible counseling prowess but this is the truth and is the true treatment needed for many.

I am NOT saying that EVERY person who is labeled as severely mentally ill can be served by this method as I have also seen the devastation a head injury, mutation, or toxic substance can render onto a person but I AM saying that there are a LOT of empaths being chemically treated and unfairly diagnosed as ill for a condition that does NOT truly exist as the macro-culture's "treatment plan" is not conducive to higher spirituality or, in any way, enlightened as the methods deployed tend to be barbaric carryovers from the days of old which postulate that all consciousness is simply the product of random synapses firing due to the effect of random chemical processes so all ailments can be treated in a manner as robotic as these inane postulates presume.

I don't believe in life after death

Neither do I... at not least in the way you are thinking about it.

There was a popular television show that seemed not to have an idea how to end so it did what many non-theists (or more aptly – those who pray at the church of science) believe... the screen suddenly went black and the show ended. The show was careful to address the fade to black as death in a previous episode and this is what the producers (and many non-theists) are programmed to believe... that you simply stop existing. The problem with this theory is thus... if you are seeing black... you EXIST.

Simply stated... the concept of non-existence CANNOT be defined or understood in human terms as ANY definition is existence. Try for a moment to imagine non-existence... what do you see? What do you feel? No matter what you see or feel the fact that you see or feel ANYTHING proves existence.

While this show ended when the main character faded to black, in another show, the main character also "died" until the character decided to stand back up. With this, you are welcome to spend as many eternities as you wish keeping your eyes closed whilst being submerged in the mud and telling yourself you do not exist or that this is simply a dream but the very act of seeing darkness or feeling empty shows existence.

As someone who actively sought the release of non-existence I am relatively skilled at imagining non-existence but, honestly, I cannot. Honestly, this is one of my favorite meditations as the energy is VERY tingly and it is reminiscent of being young and exploring certain parts of the body... touching things felt strangely compelling but there was also the question of what happens if you continue.

So while you have been programmed to simply see black and believe that all existence is gone when you die... I don't. I don't believe in death as your essence is eternal and it never does not exist. Yes you will – one day – discard your current meat puppet and return to your disincarnate life but that is all death is... a return home.

Why are empaths attracted to toxic people?

To answer this question we must define and limit some of the sweeping variables (feature engineering) as the question, otherwise, is too wide to compose a proper answer. Empaths who are in quadrant 4, for example, have absolutely no issue with toxic attraction so we know that the empath will have to be outside of quadrant 4. Quadrant 2 empaths are in perpetual empath backup and quadrant 1 empaths have their heads too far up themselves to care so neither quadrant 1 or 2 empaths are truly effected by this phenomena. Yes I am well aware that a quadrant 2 empath could attach to a toxic person and this can be (and often is) the catalyst for growth but the traditional empath/toxic relationship is found in quadrant 3 as this is a well known feature of the savior complex.

It happened to me.

My daughter's mother is an energy vampire and highly toxic. She is highly focused on her appearance and self interest and LOVES to be in crowds of people so she can consume all the free energy. I watched, in horror, her mannerisms and saw that the happier and more energetic she became (through feeding) the more people who were immediately around her began yawning and holding their head due to headaches. She sucked me in through her sob story and I allowed her to create and attach a permanent

feeding tentacle to me despite the warnings of my intuition, guides, and even my misandrist grandmother. I found I could not sleep in the same bed or room as her as doing so was draining.

What was her attraction to me? My light.

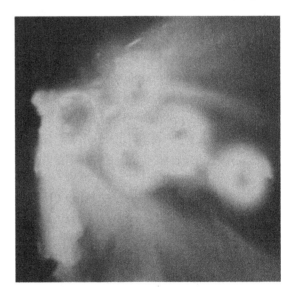

Here is a picture of my finger energy as taken by a professional Kirlian photographer. I have not shown many people this picture before and I recall the surprise of the photographer when the picture developed as the angel is rare and the photographer was VERY surprised by the solidity and brightness of my recorded energy since the mask I wear when surrounded by people is one that purposely repels people. While the photographer and the readers may be surprised by the picture, this is what attracted and attached the vampire to me as she was able to see the energy clearly and saw a strong and unending meal ticket – both financially and energetically.

I didn't sign up for this

You did and YOU are wholly and solely (or more aptly souly) responsible for everything that has happened to you and, more importantly, how you respond to whatever happens. NOTHING can happen to you without your permission. Your permission is likely to not have come from a "human" perspective as you are truly NOT human. You are, as the popular cliché teaches, an immortal spiritual being having a human experience so while you may curse whatever deity you believe in – or don't believe in – the truth remains that you are truly cursing yourself and the decisions you made prior to your human experience.

I did not choose my family

Unfortunately, you did. Depending on your level of awareness, you either selected your family personally or your prelife team selected your family with you. Either way, you did. This does not mean, however, that you have to like or get along with your "family".

As incarnated humans, we put a LOT of value and reverence in the familiar structure regarding roles as de facto but the truth is that we are ALL the same so such structure that we give so much attention to is temporary and is composed of souls who are there to assist in setting the stage for your growth. So your parents in this experience may have been your children in another or they may have played other roles. Either way, biological family is a temporary prejudice who are there for your growth.

Did you ever see your demon again?

Yes. My demon made itself known again when I was down and doing what was needed to be done to survive. A foster brother and I were homeless and living on the streets of Anchorage. A business we were working for had given us permission to sleep in the boiler room should the need ever arise... it did. It was a cold and icy night and sleeping in the park was not an option due to the freezing rain and dropping temperatures. It was later at night and we decided to sleep in the boiler room instead of walking several more blocks to a homeless shelter.

The boiler room was very warm and a welcome reprieve from the arctic air outside but it was VERY dusty and I found myself wondering what the dust was composed of. I never found out as the nearly solid embodiment of my demon materialized in front of me and intensely stared. The materialization was enough to make me reconsider the current "lodging" conditions so my foster brother and I were soon back in the arctic air heading towards an open homeless shelter for the night.

The next time I saw my demon was on the big screen. I went to see a movie that I did not know much about and nearly chocked in surprise when the main character in the movie began a battle against three demons and the main one looked nearly identical to mine! As this was a movie and the plot had to move forward, the main character dispatched of the demons relatively quickly and easily but seeing my demon friend on the big screen mirrored nearly identical to my experiences was highly synchronistic and I took the unexpected sighting as a message letting me know that it was real as was all of my experiences.

Since that time, however, I have not seen my demon.

—————————— **What do you mean you spoke to a snake before?** ——————————

Christian mythology teaches that the Christian God determined that man was growing too fast and decided to limit such growth by confusing man's languages. Such an act does not seem very loving or benevolent to me but I digress. The same mythology also states that at one point in mankind's history, mankind was able to understand all of creation... such does NOT state that man spoke the same language but the man was able to understand all of creation. It is my position and MY experience that such communicative skill is NOT lost to mankind as it is a simple matter of speaking your native tongue.

So what, then, is your native tongue? Your native tongue is the same thing you are... ENERGY or more aptly... your thoughts.

For those who know, ALL of existence is a part of you and how it responds or treats you is a direct mirror of your true thoughts and feelings. That being the case, EVERYTHING in existence is able and willing to communicate with you if you simply allow it.

There is NO "language" in Spirit as language, as we understand it, is a symbolic representation of "reality" that a society agrees upon and utilizes to express ideas but manmade language is, at best, clumsy as it is in constant flux which makes its usage extremely easy to miscommunicate and misinterpret via factors including volume, accent, translation, and visual cues among a gaggle of more technical factors.

Speaking your native tongue is a language that is understood universally and innately and is without the innumerable limitations and challenges of "modern" language.

Here are some personal examples:

- As outlined previously, I worked mainly in the crisis stabilization ward but would be temporarily moved to the prison ward, as needed, of a private psychiatric hospital in which my clientele were people who were actively homicidal, suicidal, manic, and/or in severe psychosis. Some of the clients were simply unable to communicate verbally but, very quickly, ALL of the hospital administrators noticed that I was always able to handle such clients without use of force and they all seemed to gravitate towards me for reasons the administrators could not understand. There was no secret to my success... I simply stopped listening with my ears / brain and listened, instead, with my heart.

- In another example, I was on a lawn mower cutting about 2.5 acres of grass in the midst of a summer day and was bored and hot so I decided to kick the mower in to a higher gear to get the job done faster. I was having a GRAND time cutting the grass in high speed when suddenly I was overcome with the feeling of terror. What the hell?!? I looked around and all I could see what a pine cone in front of me and wondered, "How am I feeling terror from a pine cone?" when suddenly, and before my conscious mind understood, I realized it was NOT a pine cone and took evasive action to prevent hitting the baby turtle that was dangerously close to the mower's fast spinning and unforgiving blades. Despite nearly crashing in to a tree in order to not hit the baby turtle, the baby turtle was, thankfully, unharmed albeit totally stressed out and I was able to relocate it to a safer area.

- In a final example I recall being at work when suddenly the power went out. It happens occasionally so I waited to see if is was simply a power surge or brown out and went to investigate the cause when the power did not return. All of the fuses looked good and moving switches in the fuse box did not help so I began wondering what the issue was... and then I smelled smoke. I looked outside and saw black smoke rising from a street or two over. A coworker

asked if I wanted to go there and I said yes Upon arrival it was clear that a car had driven in to a power transformer and it was completely engulfed in flame. I approached the scene in order to discern how or if I could help and found it VERY hot. I asked the fire if it intended to hurt me and it resoundingly stated no so I did what I could to assist. Many people that day thought my actions were courageous but my courage came after communicating with the fire about it's intentions.

I presented the above examples as they encompass and demonstrate communication with uncommunicative humans and communication with animals and the elements. Such examples are a VERY short list but still WELL demonstrate that you are able to communicate with ALL of existence when when you speak with your native tongue.

--------- **What are some of most blatant contradictions I have heard in a church?** ---------

To be fair, all of the following stories were heard in different sects. I will revel the denomination of the church – if I am able to recall such details – but that is as far as I will revel.

- A sister of mine was church shopping and asked me to come along to a Catholic church. She was never the religious type but was trying to fit in with a new social clique as this is where the clique leader attended. I decided to attend so that I could get the feel of another point of view but found myself somewhat disgusted by her hypocritical and chameleon-like ability to imitate all of the mannerisms and statements of those who attend

regularly... and then I listened to the sermon.

- One of the basic tenants of the Christian religion is that suicide is a cardinal sin and committing the unforgivable blight of suicide is an automatic and unwavering trip to eternal pain, suffering, and damnation yet the priest was telling a story of a saint who had happened upon a den of lion cubs and saw that the cubs were starving so without another thought the saint flung herself off a cliff so that the lion cubs could eat. I could not believe the nonsense I was hearing as not only is the priest condoning suicide but the thoughtless saint just doomed the lion cubs to death. Mankind is VERY good at killing animals ESPECIALLY animals that kill people. It is highly likely, in this story, that at some point the den will be found and when the human bones are found... the cubs will be destroyed without mercy.

- In another story, from the same Catholic church, "God" met with the devil in "God's" smoking room and "God" directed the devil to a curio that was prominently perched on a shelf above "God's" fireplace. The devil eyed the curiosity and found it to be a snow globe at which "God" lamented that this is where he kept the most loyal and faithful souls. WHAT?!? I could not believe that ANYONE would say that the BEST reward in ALL of existence was to be an item in "God's" snow globe! That is the ultimate reward for all of the nonsense? Who would buy this tripe, I contemplated, as the congregation stated an affirmative response in well trained unison and I never went back.

- I was in a church in Michigan and all seemed well. The sermon was nice and the people seemed friendly. I was invited to the group meeting and all was good until a well respected member of the church spoke. The man told of how he and his family went to the lake over the weekend and of the wonderful food and time they shared. No problem there but then he continued and mentioned that a black family arrived at the lake and parked next to him. No problem there, I thought, until I heard his horrific and unreasonable response to this innocent act... he went to his car and got a baseball bat out of the trunk and "convinced" the black family to go somewhere else! I IMMEDIATELY

left and NEVER returned to this house of horrors.

- I was in a Southern Baptist church in Florida and witnessed a Hellspawn in the church who was praised and coddled regardless of action. The Hellspawn acted with impunity and seemed to be immune to all consequences and the leaders of the church's social group accepted every deviant act with praise and adoration. I eventually left the church and, some time later, found that the Hellspawn's impunity had expired and the Hellspawn had been sentenced to a LOT of time in prison for several counts of vehicular manslaughter whilst on another DUI. I neither condone the growth lessons of the Hellspawn nor condemn the Hellspawn for the same and went back to the church to simply ask them to pray for the Hellspawn as, I would imagine, the reality of the growth lesson and the sentence is enough to quash the spirit of anyone... nothing doing. I was dismayed and angered that the same people who had a MAJOR influence on the eventual fall of the Hellspawn were too high and mighty to EVEN pray for THEIR manifestation but... they were happy that I was back. HELL NO!!!

- It should be noted that the Hellspawn is actually the person who got me in to church and we attended quite a few activities together – including youth group.

The youth group took a mission trip one summer and both me and the Hellspawn were in attendance. While taking a break from traveling, we came to a mountainous overpass in which the drop was quite large and, most likely, not survivable. The Hellspawn made it a point to stand on a very precarious ledge overlooking the potential free-fall. In seeing him in this position, the youth pastor gestured to me that I should push him off as no one would miss him. So here was someone who was supposed to be encouraging the youth to achieve Christian "ideals" yet here he was encouraging me to murder a fellow parishioner stating no one would miss the person. I was appalled and kept this quiet.

For the record, upon returning from the youth mission, that youth minister was fired for misappropriation of church funds.

- I was working for a small technology company in Georgia and wanted to get better acquainted with the community so I decided to attend a Baptist church that had a good reputation. It was the Fourth of July weekend so, naturally, the sermon gravitated towards the United States and freedom. I purposely turned my cell phone off so not to disturb anyone before entering the church and was behaving and not challenging the propaganda laden sermon. I listened to the preacher express his LOVE for freedom and how thankful he is to live in the US but all this ended with his NEXT statement.

I was dismayed and dumbfounded when the preacher followed his long winded and logical fallacy laden dissertation on his love of freedom with "All Christians are the property of Jesus Christ." WHAT?!? Apparently I was the ONLY person in the ENTIRE congregation that heard this fool lament about his LOVE of freedom and – IN

THE SAME BREATH – joyfully call himself a SLAVE. My answer came in a resounding Amen to which I had to find a way out before I caused a scene. Thankfully, as I was beginning to clear my voice in order to present a dissenting opinion, my cell phone began to ring which gave me the perfect excuse to leave but to my surprise, the cell phone was still OFF when I tried to answer it in the lobby!

- I was in Orlando and having breakfast at a restaurant near the headquarters of religious organization. At this point I, honestly, cannot recall the sect and I cannot seem to find it on Google maps.

Regardless, church representatives took new adepts to the restaurant to chat with them about the tenants of their faith. I, of course, could not mind my own business so I eavesdropped and overheard the representative stating that they do not believe or teach the dogma of Hell. I did my best not to scoff too loudly but my disdain for the comment was noticed so I continued and questioned how they sold their nonsense.

My comment was not well received but I was genuinely interested on how they expected to grow their business by removing their main marketing point. Let's be honest, what the church sells is NOT eternal life, unconditional love, or helping those in need but it sells salvation from Hell. Listen to MANY church hymns and they all have the same general theme, they love Christ not because Christ is a wonderful teacher who believes that you can do the same as him – AND more – but because the sales pitch of the church is that Christ will save you from Hell.

This is Marketing 101 and is best understood simply by the marketer releasing a public service education program in which the fear based product is introduced and promoted and then sell the product. Unfortunately, my sincere question fell "upon deaf ears" and the representative continued on albeit somewhat irritated at my audacity.

Why must we forget when we incarnate?

The quick and easy answer is so that you can focus on your current experience.

ALL of us have had previous experiences in which we have done things that were needed to be done for the fulfillment of that experience but which we may find reprehensible now. It is likely that the person will attach a "modern" paradigm to their past actions they undertook in the previous experience to overcome those growth challenges and suffer a malady of emotions as a result of their memories. While, technically, you ARE the same being you were in your previous experiences, you are NOT the product of those growth challenge choices unless you allow yourself to be and since most are still learning to exist in their current bevy of growth challenges... it is best NOT to overwhelm the current experience with ghosts of the past.

This does not mean, however, that you are completely free of the ghosts of the past as people can relive such scenes in their dreams and become stuck. Of course being able to see the past in dreams or in "awakened" recall are challenges afforded to those who are able to handle and address such challenges. It is VERY easy to find stories of counselors accidentally entering in to the realm of past life regressions and the healing that can be obtained when nothing else seems to work.

While those who subscribe to the religion of science will balk at this wisdom and poo-poo it all of the voluminous examples to the domain of placebo – a realm they cannot understand or control so they do all they can to dismiss it – this is, nonetheless, the very essence of healing. Healing is NOT obtained by hiding from or doing everything you can to detour from your challenges... healing is obtained by facing your demons, diseases, and other "bad" things you grant life and power to by your hatred or fear of them. Of course, a rest period is often the key and this is why techniques, including past life regression, work as facing the challenges from a safe, removed distance is often the key to allowing you to explore the lesson from a different perspective and "exercise" the challenge so that it can deliver its wisdom to you – the same wisdom YOU asked for and it has been attempting to deliver – and become unblocked.

So, in summary, you incarnate with "amnesia" so that you can set the stage to obtain the "level" needed to successfully complete the growth challenges you selected regardless of when or where the origin of such challenges were originally requested.

What is Gleipnir?

As someone who spent a good deal of my young childhood analyzing different cultures, religions, and perspectives, I read a lot and found I really enjoyed the stories of the Norse which is better known to most as Norse Mythology. I found the Norse stories to be more realistic than those of the Greek or Roman flavors; although, admittedly, there are a LOT of parallels among the great mythologies of yesteryear. I know the reader may not like this point but it is VERY easy to see the mythological "gods" of the old religions in the Saints of "modern" day religion. I could get lost in the blatant comparisons but that would easily be an entire series onto itself so I will regain the focus of this section.

In Norse Mythology, Gleipnir is the rope-like cloth the Gods commissioned the dwarves to create in order to bind Loki's eldest child, Fenrir. The dwarves had crafted some of the "God's" most powerful weapons in prior commissions and Gleipnir was no exception as Wikipedia ("Gleipnir". 2018. En.Wikipedia. Org. https://en.wikipedia.org/wiki/Gleipnir) revels Gleipnir was composed of:

- The sound of a cat's footfall
- The beard of a woman
- The roots of a mountain
- The sinews of a bear
- The breath of a fish
- The spittle of a bird

Unlike the moronic mythology of the biblical strongman Sampson – Sampson was queried about the source of his strength and found that each answer was attacked but Sampson (blinded by love or lust) never caught on, Fenrir was wise as he suspected the "Gods" were attempting to bind him as this was not the first "binding" they "Gods" challenged Fenrir to break. Fenrir demanded a good will gesture to prove the "Gods" weren't trying to trick him so Tyr placed his hand in Fenrir's mouth and Fenrir promptly severed it when Fenrir found that Gleipnir was impossible to break and he was bound.

Who Cares Analysis	There is a lot happening in this aptly named section which was introduced as a way to summarize some of the most commonly asked questions I have asked or have had asked of me over my experience. There is something in this section to challenge the programming of everyone no matter where they are on the Spiritual Time Clock but especially for those in quadrants I and II.

CONCLUSION

I want the thank those who found their way to this book. There is a lot of information and ideas conveyed throughout the pages of this tome and the reader is sure to have experienced a myriad of emotions and colorful metaphors as my words purposefully and intentionally challenged your programming, cognitive dissonance, and "reality".

I do not have all the answers and I can only present my medicine to you throughout the filters and biases of my current experience. I have taken pains to make the contents of this book thought provoking while keeping names, details, and my ego based biases to a minimum in the sincere hope that those who are darkened will find solace in this book as they learn that they are in control no matter what the circumstance.

As an empath, healer, seer, reader, psydude (sorry I am not a chic), student, teacher, etc., who is able to see the big picture, I know that time and "reality" is an illusion and despite the challenges we allow ourselves to experience, we are all the same and are all safe at "home". There is NO "perfection" to obtain, no barrier to entry, and no limit to the love we receive except for the limitations we accept. Yes, we can get lost in our experiences but that simply underscores the creative power and freedom all of us have. No, you are NOT "granted" free will as such grant implies a slave/master relationship which only exists if you allow yourself to resonate with it. As far as I can tell… the ONLY things that are impossible are (1) understanding nothingness and (2) seeing outside of the collective and universal energy that is colloquially called God but, then again, I do not know everything.

I sincerely wish you the best on your journey and growth and hope that you were able to find some nugget of information within the pages of this book to help you overcome a sticking point, achieve something more than you ever allowed yourself to think possible, or embrace and understand the Blessings of the Dark!

Printed in the United States
By Bookmasters